# "Keep the Ball a Rolling"

## A Pictorial History of Claremont Country Club

### 1903–2003

by

J. Parry Wagener

The Donning Company/Publishers

184 Business Park Drive, Suite 206

Virginia Beach, VA 23462

Steve Mull, General Manager

Barbara B. Buchanan, Office Manager

Barbara Bolton, Project Director

Anne Cordray, Project Research Coordinator

Jan Martin, Senior Copyeditor/Production Coordinator

Lori Wiley, Designer

Scott Rule, Director of Marketing

Travis Gallup, Marketing Coordinator

Library of Congress Cataloging-in-Publication Data

Wagener, J. Parry, 1937–
    Keep the ball a rolling : a pictorial history of Claremont Country Club, 1903–2003 / by J. Parry Wagener.
        p. cm.
    Includes index.
    ISBN 1–57864–201–9
    1. Claremont Country Club (Oakland, Calif.)—History. 2. Golf—California—Oakland—History. 3. Tennis—California—Oakland—History. I. Title.

GV969.C53 W33 2003
796.352'06—dc21

2002041109

Printed in the United States of America

(© Joann Dost)

(© Joann Dost)

TABLE OF CONTENTS

(© Joann Dost)

(© Joann Dost)

3

In 1998 I offered to produce a map that would describe the 1903 land acquisitions that formed Claremont Country Club. That information was discovered accidentally while researching early tax rolls for the Piedmont Historical Society. I had no idea that project would lead to the enormous history program that has evolved over the last five years. With the early encouragement of the Board of Directors, Alec Churchward, and John Fite, I soon found myself completely hooked on the acquisition and preservation of the record of Claremont Country Club and its one-hundred-year history. From the earliest call to members and friends and through the research of numerous helpers, the archives of the Club have exploded with documents, photos, trophies, maps, books, and other memorabilia too diverse to mention.

At the same time as the archives were growing, the Board of Directors appointed a Centennial Chairman, Kent Penwell, who with his various committees began to plan the 2003 Centennial Celebration. A history book was discussed, but there had already been two histories produced: one in 1960 by former President Frank Barnett, and a second well-written, expanded, hardcover account in 1988 by Robert Patmont. At first, another history book did not seem to me to be necessary; however, it soon became apparent that we were collecting a mountain of visual data in addition to new historic information. Thus, it was these events that provided the impetus to publish a pictorial history, one that could truly provide additional information and, hopefully, a visual life to the fine work of the earlier authors. The title of this book, *"Keep the Ball a Rolling,"* was the motto of Claremont's predecessor, the Oakland Golf Club, which figures prominently in this publication. Many of the early golf and country clubs had clever mottos, and their members value them today as much as they value their club's formal name. *"Keep the Ball a Rolling"* is intended to preserve that important aspect of our past.

The credit for this book goes to many, because I have had wonderful assistance in both the archiving and writing processes. In addition to the people mentioned above, I want to specifically thank a few others. First, the whole project would not have been possible without the tireless assistance of Bruce Hayes, who during the last five years provided enormous support. Much credit also belongs to John Fite, who not only encouraged people to share memorabilia but also researched history in libraries and at historic golf sites such as Carnoustie, Scotland, and the USGA Headquarters in Far Hills, New Jersey. Our book committee— the people that spent hours selecting and editing information—consisted of Bruce Hayes, Kathy Burden, Judy Jones, and Gini Ragsdale. All deserve special recognition, as do several people involved with our photography, including Susan Mangas, Peter Bush, Joann Dost, and Sarah Joplin. The Board of Directors also should be recognized for its ongoing encouragement of the project and for its critical financial support. Finally, I want to thank the staff at the Northern California Golf Association, Richard Janusch, Aldo Galletti, Dr. Gary Nelson, Gail Lombardi, Eureka Cartography, and the historians at many local clubs for both their input and advice.

As volunteers, we have tried to present this history as accurately as possible, yet we are mindful that errors and omissions may have occurred. We hope you enjoy what we have presented and ask for your understanding should something be amiss.

**Author**

Facing page: *"Steelehead" golf clubs were custom-made at Claremont during the 1930s by assistant golf professional Howard Steele.*
*(© Joann Dost)*

Left: *The "George Nicoll" Scottish-made putter was used by title-winning Claremont golfer Stuart Hawley Jr.*
*(© Joann Dost)*

The One Hundredth Anniversary of Claremont Country Club is truly a milestone. The Club's many generations of members have experienced all the joys and the tragedies that any single century could possibly offer. During this time period, the automobile, telephone, television, and computer have been invented. Antibiotics, human transplants, and moon landings have all become realities. We have experienced major earthquakes, epidemics, fires, and the continuation of armed conflicts that range from wars to terrorism. Yet, somehow we remain fortunate to live in a free country and to enjoy all manner of blessings, including the bond of friendship that prevails at Claremont Country Club. Our Club is truly a unique place for rest, relaxation, sport, and camaraderie.

Plans for the Centennial Celebration have been in the works for nearly three years. The Steering Committee and several special-events committees have sorted through many ideas and numerous budgets to provide the members with meaningful centennial memories. The celebration will include special member events and three separate documentaries, the first of which is the centennial calendar.

The second is the pictorial history that you are now reading, which is the culmination of five years of researching, archiving, selecting, and writing to capture the essence of the Club and its past activities. Lastly, a centennial video is being produced to augment the pictorial history and to provide each member with a slightly different perspective of certain segments of our history. With these keepsakes, the committee hopes to provide each member with a truly memorable centennial experience that may be enjoyed for years to come.

I consider it an honor and a privilege to serve as Claremont's Centennial Chairman, and I feel fortunate to have such a wonderful group of men and women serving on our Centennial Committee. All have given graciously of their time and their experience to help make the centennial year a success. In addition, Alec Churchward and his staff are to be recognized for their support and hard work in helping to plan our centennial events.

I would particularly like to acknowledge and thank Parry Wagener, our historian. Words cannot adequately express my appreciation of Parry's donation of time, insight, and meticulous work on the archives and the writing of this pictorial history. Without him, this book would not have been possible.

This centennial history book is dedicated to the individuals who had the foresight to establish Claremont Country Club and to the members—past and present—in whose hands our history was so ably molded and our traditions were preserved. Our future, thanks to them, seems ensured. We should all be proud to be a part of Claremont's first one hundred years. May the second one hundred be twice as good!

M. Robert Pennell

Centennial Chairman

# CLAREMONT'S ROOTS
## —THE OAKLAND GOLF CLUB

## CHAPTER 1

Oakland Golf Club.

**Above:** *Logo and motto of the Oakland Golf Club, which was founded in 1897 and was the predecessor of Claremont Country Club.*

**Facing page:** *The earliest known photograph of the Oakland Golf Club's grounds on the opposite shore of Lake Merritt, circa 1902. A. P. Harmon's house and garden are shown in the foreground. The Ordway Building, parking lot, and Harrison Street occupy Harmon's property today.*

Claremont Country Club was originally founded as the Oakland Golf Club in 1897. On December 10 of that year, a group of twenty business leaders formally agreed to donate a fund of two thousand dollars to establish the Oakland Golf Club by Lake Merritt in the Adams Point area of Oakland, California. The agreement stated the purpose of the fund was as follows.

*With a view of increasing the Social Life of Oakland and rescuing it from the lethargy in which it seems to have fallen, it has been proposed to start the ball a rolling by the formation of a Golf Club, following the example set by so many places in the East and West during the past season, where the formation of like Clubs has had a most remarkable success; meeting with the spontaneous and hearty approval of the people.*

The Oakland Golf Club thus joined its predecessors— Burlingame Country Club, which was organized in 1893 with a three-hole course, and San Francisco Golf Club, which was organ-

*Right: Francis Marion "Borax" Smith was one of Oakland Golf Club's more colorful members.*

*Below: The original founding agreement for Oakland Golf Club was signed in 1897 by many prominent men of the Bay Area community.*

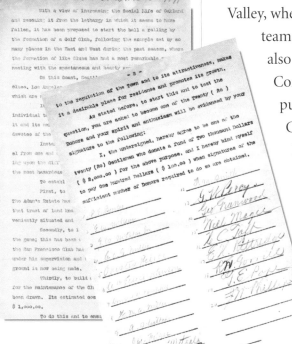

ized in 1895 with a nine-hole course at the present-day site of Presidio Golf Club—as the only golf clubs in the Bay Area.

Francis Marion Smith was a principal supporter of the new golf venture and a strong believer in the future of Oakland. He was a powerful figure who was better known as "Borax" Smith, because he made a fortune from his borax mine in Death Valley, where the famous twenty-mule teams hauled the ore to market. He also controlled the East Bay Water Company, formed the Key System public-transit network, and built the Claremont Hotel in partnership with Frank C. Havens. Smith and Havens also formed The Realty Syndicate, which owned or controlled large amounts of East Bay land, including most of the property upon which the future Claremont Country Club would be built.

On January 3, 1898, Smith wrote a letter to Philip E. Bowles, president of the First National Bank of Oakland. In it he stated one of the principles he felt was basic to the formation of the Oakland Golf Club: *It is time that we had a*

*"City" in the place of the "Village" of Oakland. We want a large and popular Golf Club.* In addition to Smith and Bowles, other prominent signatories to the agreement included George McNear, Orestes Pierce, C. O. G. Miller, J. A. Folger, and George Greenwood.

The location of Oakland Golf Club was Adams Point, a peninsula that jutted into the north end of the tidal basin that was then known as San Antonio Slough and is now known as Lake Merritt. Today the area is called Lakeside Park. The top priority of the new golf club was the construction of both a clubhouse and golf links. The founding agreement of 1897 stated, *The services of the expert of the San Francisco Club has been engaged and the Links laid out under his supervision.* This expert was identified as William Robertson, the first golf professional in northern California. Not only did he lay out the Oakland links, he also planned San Francisco Golf Club's links at the Presidio and the links at San Rafael Golf Club, which opened in 1898. After the Oakland golf course was completed, a clubhouse was constructed at the present-day site of the Lakeside Park bandstand. According to the *Overland Monthly, The Oakland Golf Club occupies about a hundred acres of picturesque land dotted with graceful oaks, at Adams Point, which juts out into Lake Merritt. The clubhouse stands on a knoll and*

*Oakland Golf Club was originally located at Adams Point, part of which is now Lakeside Park. Streets such as Grand Avenue (which appear in the shaded area) were built after the Club was removed. (© Eureka Cartography)*

**Right:** *The original clubhouse at Oakland Golf Club is shown with the first tee-box in the middle foreground.*

**Opposite page:** *Clubhouse veranda. The woman in the white dress is believed to be Mrs. Bruegger, the club stewardess.*

*Earliest known scenes of play at Oakland Golf Club, circa 1899.*
*Golf photographs from the early days of Oakland Golf Club Club show a very*
*different style of attire.* Top left: *Arthur Goodall (left)*; bottom left: *George S.*
*Wheaton (left) and A. P. Brayton (center)*; above: *William Pierce Johnson.*

14

Whether there were nine, fourteen, or eighteen holes, play went east along the lake and then north toward the hills. Between the first and second tees, players hiked along a cow trail that later would become Grand Avenue. *Harper's Official Golf Guide* described the course as *laid out over rolling country, with all grass putting greens.* It is not surprising that Oakland Golf Club was an immediate success.

Left: *Thomas Rickard putting;* above: *Harry J. Knowles.*

15

*Earliest known scenes of play at Oakland Golf Club, circa 1899. Above: John A. McNear; right: Sam Bell McKee (left), caddie wearing a bowler hat (center), and Louis Monteagle (right).*

Left: *C. Hutchinson (left), caddie (center), and Robert Fitzgerald (right)*; above: *Robert Fitzgerald (left) and C. Hutchinson.*

commands an extensive view . . . The captain of the Oakland Golf Club is Orestes Pierce, and its vice-captain is P. E. Bowles.

Most reports from this time period refer to the Oakland Golf Club as a nine-hole golf course, although the 1901 edition of *Harper's Official Golf Guide* lists eighteen holes with a total of 4,074 yards. On the other hand, the *Overland Monthly* wrote,

*There is a short course of 1,184 yards, and a long one of 2,890 yards. . . . It is not quite strictly a full eighteen-hole course, as there are only fourteen greens; but these are all of good turf, well rolled, and kept in excellent trim.*

Area newspapers reported the first local tournaments that involved Oakland Golf Club members, including quite a few tournaments between Oakland Golf Club and San Francisco Golf Club. The rivalry between the opposite sides of the bay was keenly felt, as competitors played for the honor of bringing home a silver

*Facing page: Another view of Oakland Golf Club's grounds and clubhouse from across Lake Merritt in A. P. Harmon's garden, circa 1899*

*Left: Home-and-Home Trophy from tournament between Oakland Golf Club and San Francisco Golf Club, circa 1902*

*Below: Oakland Golf Club Handicap Tournament trophy won by William Pierce Johnson in 1900 (© Joann Dost)*

Above: *James Melville, Oakland
Golf Club's first golf professional*

Opposite page, left: *Horace Rawlins,
winner of the first U.S. Open in 1895, was
Oakland Golf Club's second professional.*

Opposite page, right: *Willie Anderson served as
Oakland Golf Club's instructor during Horace
Rawlins' tenure. He went on to win the U.S. Open
four times in 1901, 1903, 1904, and 1905.*

cup to display at their clubs. It was from these competitive meetings, which also included Burlingame Country Club and San Rafael Golf Club, that the Northern California Golf Association (NCGA) was formed in 1901. In the NCGA's recent centennial history, Claremont Country Club is listed as one of the association's founders, since it succeeded the Oakland Golf Club.

Oakland Golf Club's first golf professional was James Melville, a golfer from Scotland who worked on ranches and railroads in the United States until 1897. An interesting anecdotal story, which was related twenty-seven years later by Robert Fitzgerald and appeared in *Fairway Magazine*, described how Melville was hired:

> One afternoon in the year 1898, a group of us were gathered in front of the clubhouse when an unmistakable cowboy sauntered up and asked if we wanted a professional for the club. Somewhat amused, one of the members asked him if he knew anything about golf. He drawled a reply to the effect that he knew plenty. "Here, take this club and see if you can hit a ball," said the member. As soon as the cowboy took hold of the club we realized it was an implement familiar to his hands. He drove such a beautiful ball in such beautiful form that we hired him on the spot. It seems that he had been riding the range for several years and that the call of the links had brought him into town looking for a job at his original calling.

Melville moved on to become the professional at Burlingame Country Club and later at the Hotel Del Monte at Monterey. John D. Motion, a former greenskeeper at Chicago Golf Club, followed Melville for a brief stint. In 1899 Horace Rawlins, winner of the first U.S. Open in 1895, was hired as the professional at Oakland Golf Club. He was very popular and was sought after for his teaching skills. Rawlins hired Willie Anderson of Baltusrol Golf Club in Springfield, New Jersey, to serve as a golf instructor. Anderson was a crack golfer by the age of twenty, when he placed second in the 1897 U.S. Open. He went on to win the U.S. Open four times in 1901, 1903, 1904, and 1905.

While the Adams Point site was an ideal location for attracting members from around the area, its location near the center of the city also made the property prime real estate. One news article in the *Oakland Tribune* summed up the situation by writing, *The golf days of Adam's Point are numbered. That beautiful section is to be turned into home sites for men of means and cultivated tastes.* At the end of 1902, the members of Oakland Golf Club faced the choice of forming a new club or crossing San Francisco Bay to play golf. The Club's directors decided to remain in the East Bay area and began a search for new property outside the city limits.

2869 – Claremont Country Club, Oakland, California

## CLAREMONT'S INCORPORATION
## AND EARLY DAYS

On January 27, 1903, a group of twenty-five men from Oakland and the surrounding area, most of whom were members of the vanishing Oakland Golf Club, filed articles of incorporation for Claremont Country Club with the California Secretary of State. The general purposes of the corporation were to *promote social intercourse among, and to furnish pleasure, happiness and health to its members.*
The specific objectives of the new organization were as follows:

> *To foster, encourage, promote, advance and create interest in and the practice of and enjoyment of golf, lawn tennis, baseball, football, lacrosse, steeple chasing,*

Above: *Claremont's first oak tree logo was adopted in 1905, when the Board of Directors proclaimed the official colors of the Club would be red and green.*

Left: *Claremont's Articles of Incorporation, January 27, 1903 (© Joann Dost)*

Facing page: *Postcard view of the clubhouse, circa early 1900s (© Joann Dost)*

*To help finance the Club during the early days, life memberships were sold to twenty-five members of the community for one thousand dollars each.*

*hare and hounds, bowling, polo, trap shooting, pigeon shooting, riding, driving, billiards and all other outdoor and indoor sports.*

An article in the March 14, 1903, issue of the *Oakland Enquirer* announced plans for the new country club that promised *something quite swell*. When the Club was incorporated, the members had an option to purchase 125 acres of land in the Claremont District that were owned by the Edson Adams estate; when that option fell through, a second site in Rock Ridge Township was purchased. This site had 107 acres of land and included the large H. P. Livermore residence, which was located on the site of Claremont's present-day clubhouse. Most of the property was acquired from The Realty Syndicate, and several adjacent parcels were purchased from two private individuals.

It is interesting to speculate on the Club's name. Both parcels of land that were under consideration were located beyond Oakland city limits; thus, keeping the name Oakland Golf Club was not considered. The first optioned land was in the Claremont District, which is why the name Claremont was used in the Articles of Incorporation. When the option was not exercised, one might think the name Rock Ridge Country Club would have been considered; however, it may have required too much effort and expense to revise the incorporation certificate. No matter the reason, the name Claremont was retained.

The new Club was to be much larger and grander than the Oakland Golf Club. Under California law at that time, corporations were forbidden to own more than fifty acres of land. To avoid this law, many clubs incorporated as nonprofit entities, but rather than incorporate as a nonprofit corporation, the founders of Claremont Country Club came up with a unique solution. Three of the founders—William Pierce Johnson, Edwin Goodall, and Robert M. Fitzgerald—purchased fifty acres in their names, and their land was adjacent to the fifty acres that were purchased by the Club. Construction on the combined lands was put on hold until founding member Frederick Stratton, a state legislator, was able to pass a bill that annulled land limitations for corporations.

Claremont Country Club's property was part of a grant made in 1820 by the King of Spain to Luis Maria Peralta. The original grant covered forty-eight thousand acres, which were spread over the present-day areas of Oakland, Berkeley, Piedmont, Alameda, and part of San Leandro. In 1842 Peralta divided his empire among his four sons. Vicente Peralta received the land that extends from present-day downtown Oakland to Berkeley. Ten years later he sold a portion that included the Club's site to a group that was led by Colonel John C. Hayes, the first sheriff of San Francisco. The Hayes group then sold the Rock Ridge site to Horatio Gates Livermore and his two sons. For many years the three Livermores occupied spacious homes near the Club's present-day property. In the 1880s one of the sons, Horatio

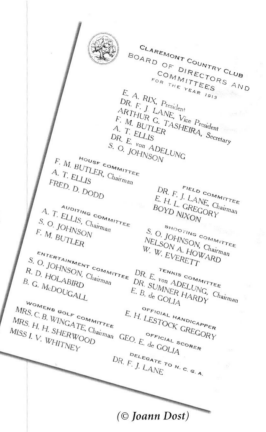

*(© Joann Dost)*

Putnam Livermore, built a palatial home above where Broadway Terrace and the 16th fairway are located today.

In 1891 Philip E. Bowles, a founding member of both the Oakland and Claremont Clubs, acquired fifty acres that included H. P. Livermore's thirty-eight-room residence. Bowles asked Livermore to move his home so that Bowles could construct his own mansion on the property. During the early 1890s, Livermore's large home was moved to the present-day clubhouse site, and in 1903 the house became Claremont's first clubhouse.

It took a lot of work and nearly two years to get Claremont Country Club from incorporation to opening day. The founders had a long and complicated job of financing and developing the property to make certain the new Claremont Country Club had more amenities than the Oakland Golf Club. Plans for expanding the kitchen and constructing a new dining room, locker rooms, and a ballroom with bowling alleys below were initiated.

According to a May 9, 1904, *Oakland Tribune* article, *Forty men are now clearing grounds for a golf course. They are in the main felling trees along a line which will extend through the eastern section of the lands, thence to the north and, finally to the west, terminating in what is known as Thermal Vale.* There also were plans for constructing two tennis courts.

Many of the members of Claremont Country Club came from the membership of Oakland Golf Club, but the new facility was built to handle a larger group. To develop a larger membership, lists were drawn up of prospective East Bay members from Alameda, Oakland, and Berkeley.

Claremont was ready for its official opening on December 3, 1904, and invitations were sent out to four hundred members and six hundred guests. For one of the opening events, a five-hundred-dollar budget covered the expenses of a lunch of cold meats, salad, and refreshments that was served to an estimated five hundred guests.

When Claremont opened, many of Oakland's streets were

*The entrance to Claremont Country Club at the top of Clifton Street. (© Joann Dost)*

unpaved, including Broadway. Most transportation was by foot, horse, or horse-drawn carriage. Streetcar service ran from Fortieth Street along Broadway to Clifton, and from there one had to continue one long block up a hill to get to the Club. The original main entrance to Claremont, which was flanked by two stone pillars, was approached from the top of Clifton Street through the present-day pool parking lot. According to a March 14, 1903, *Oakland Enquirer* article, *The incorporators have the assurance of the Transit Company that its street car lines will be extended to the entrance to the grounds so they can be reached quickly and easily.*

To facilitate the transportation, *Large stables have been fitted up and installed with attendants to care for the conveyances of the guests.* The unpaved roads did not hamper attendance at the grand opening.

The new facility received rave reviews in the local press, and the *Oakland Enquirer* ran a half-page article that extolled the virtues of the Club.

*Poised high on the apex of a hill, the artistically constructed club house towers above the surrounding undulating hills and valleys in majestic serenity. No more ideal site could have been selected for a club building . . . Large airy rooms for members, richly fitted up with private baths attached, occupy the second and third floors, while the first floor has well-appointed drawing rooms, billiard and card rooms, reading rooms, and dining room and a most completely outfitted kitchen . . . the opening today . . . is one of the most eventful days in social club circles in California.*

Club President Edwin Goodall summed up the state of the Club in his "President's Report" during the members' first annual meeting on February 1, 1906. He described the efforts of those members who had established the new Club in the East Bay.

*I am almost persuaded that could those who were instrumental in starting that movement have foreseen the length of time and the amount of work and worry necessary to make it a success—even the brilliant success that it is today—they would have hesitated long before assuming the responsibilities of the undertaking.*

Many of the organizers of the new Club were willing to go back to San Francisco for golf if the organization's attempt failed; however, Goodall reported some rather astonishing statistics about Claremont's new membership.

*It may interest you to know that of the 389 members, Oakland furnishes 187, San Francisco 98, Berkeley 65, Alameda 29 and various other localities 10. It therefore appears that by reason of the successful establishment of this Club, Oakland not only held as residents many of the members of the old Oakland Golf Club, who would have otherwise moved to the city, but that the threatened ebb tide was*

Above: *Original clubhouse*

Facing page: *Edwin Goodall, Claremont's first President, was one of the founders who helped purchase the land that Claremont Country Club stands on today.*

*actually turned to flood, bringing nearly a hundred residents of San Francisco as members of this Club.*

Goodall praised the first Board of Directors who were stepping down by saying, *After three years of earnest work the Board feels a sense of relief in retiring and transferring their duties to other hands and hearts less fatigued.* He then described the unusual attributes of the new Club.

> *For accessibility, or picturesqueness of location, for the stateliness and yet homelike comforts of its Club House, for the beauty of its rare flowers and its magnificent views, for the high standard of its moral atmosphere, no word of scandal ever having stained its unblemished record, for its high credit and splendid financial condition, it stands today in its youthful vigor basking in the sunshine of success and, like our own glorious State, of which it is a part, the peer of the best in the land.*

He closed his report in a rather humble, apologetic fashion by saying,

> *If in looking around you find, as you doubtless will, some evidences of omissions or commissions*

which do not meet with your unqualified approval, remember that those who have had the matters in hand are not
experts, but simply privates in the ranks [who] have freely
given much of their time and attention to the Club's affairs,
and to the warp and woof of which undertaking they have
woven their unselfish devotion.

Above: *Early-day parking lot*

Facing page: *Pedestrian path to
clubhouse from Clifton Street*

SPLENDID CONTESTS SEEN ON GROUNDS
OF CLAREMONT COUNTRY CLUB'S HOME

SCENES AT THE OPENING OF THE NEW HOME OF THE CLAREMONT COUNTRY CLUB, SHOWING THE GUESTS ON THE VERANDA OF THE CLUBHOUSE AND WATCHING THE SCOTTISH BOWLING AND GOLF CONTESTS.

Above: *The* Oakland Enquirer *covered
the official opening of Claremont
Country Club. (© Joann Dost)*

Opposite page: *Interior views
of the clubhouse (© Joann Dost)*

Goodall singled out Robert Fitzgerald for his help with the complicated acquisition of property by stating, *Mr. R. M. Fitzgerald attended to it all without cost to the Club.* Indeed, Fitzgerald had a remarkable influence on the Club during its early years. A prominent lawyer and an avid golfer from the days of Oakland Golf Club, he was with Claremont from the start and devoted years of service to an organization he loved. He was president of Claremont twice for a total of nineteen years, once in 1908 and then in 1916 for eighteen consecutive years.

Entrance fees for the new Club were one hundred dollars for men and fifty dollars for women. Dues were five dollars per month for individual members and ten dollars per month for families. In 1905 a lifetime membership at Claremont Country Club was one thousand dollars, and subscribers did not have to pay monthly dues. Until 1915 the two classes of membership—regular and life—were nonproprietary. In one instance the barter system was employed for payment of an entrance fee, which was noted in the 1904 Board minutes: *Resolved that the Club purchase from Horatio Livermore, the billiard table now at the Clubhouse for the sum of $100 to cover the entrance fee of Mr. Livermore's son, Norman, for required membership.*

Dining Room

Entrance Hall

A Bed Room

Ball Room

*Robert Fitzgerald was one of Claremont's founders and was president of the Club for nineteen years.*

The early years of Claremont were prosperous ones. Net profits for the first fourteen months were $16,077.72, nine thousand dollars of which came from the sale of a small portion of land that was not needed. The Club was fully staffed and maintained various forms of recreation for its members. There was an indoor bowling alley with two lanes in the basement of the clubhouse, and on the south side of the clubhouse, there was a lawn-bowling green, which was another popular Club activity. From the beginning women were active participants in the Club's golfing, tennis, and lawn-bowling programs. Mrs. Philip Bowles was captain of the ladies' team at Oakland Golf Club, and in 1903 she became captain of the first ladies' golf team at Claremont Country Club.

The Club needed a larger kitchen, so in 1910 the Board hired Julia Morgan, a well-known California architect, to design the new kitchen and other clubhouse alterations as well. High usage of the golf facilities required a large golf staff, and by 1920 the Club had a pool of one hundred seventy-five caddies. Members were required to use caddies, and since many members played thirty-six holes in the course of a day, particularly on weekends, many caddies were required to accommodate the heavy demand. There was a rule that a caddie could not carry for more than eighteen holes at a time without giving another caddie the opportunity to work.

During the first quarter of the century, dues were increased only twice to a maximum of fifteen dollars per month. In 1915, when William Pierce Johnson was Claremont's President, the Club changed its policy and issued proprietary memberships only. Members were issued certificates that could be sold back to the Club or sold to a person approved for membership if the owner of the certificate resigned from the Club or died. Also in 1915, the original two categories of membership were increased to seven.

The Club's decisions reflected the conservative character of its membership. In 1912 the Board of Directors recommended the acquisition of an additional six hundred acres of land near Walnut Creek as an investment in the Club's future. The merits of this proposal notwithstanding, the members turned it down. In 1936 and at the height of the Great Depression, a proposal to purchase Mt. Diablo Country Club for thirty thousand dollars also was rejected by Claremont's members.

The early years of Claremont Country Club were filled with a variety of activities. Tournaments, parties, and other Club events were held with much fanfare. One tradition that carried over from Oakland Golf Club to Claremont Country Club was the popular Home-and-Home Tournaments between local golf clubs. These tournaments were played by both the men's and ladies' teams. According to a January 1906 *Western Field Magazine* article about the ladies' team, *The contest will bring*

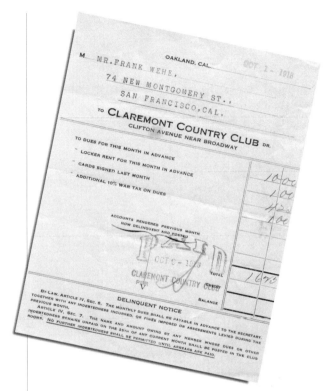

*Dues invoices show the significantly lower price for membership during the early days.*

JUNE 7 1919

MRS. C. F. FORD (left) and MRS. T. S. BAKER, snapped as they finished their match on the Claremont course yesterday. Mrs. Ford won the honors in the finals after a hard game with Mrs. Baker.

**Above:** *Unlike many other clubs during the early days, Claremont had an active ladies' golf program.*

**Facing page and left:** *Golfers show off early-day fashions. (© Joann Dost)*

37

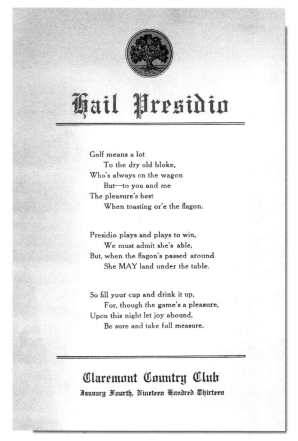

### Hail Presidio

Golf means a lot
To the dry old bloke,
Who's always on the wagon
But—to you and me
The pleasure's best
When toasting or'e the flagon.

Presidio plays and plays to win,
We must admit she's able,
But, when the flagon's passed around
She MAY land under the table.

So fill your cup and drink it up,
For, though the game's a pleasure,
Upon this night let joy abound,
Be sure and take full measure.

#### Claremont Country Club
January Fourth, Nineteen Hundred Thirteen

*Early-day menus and invitations*

**Opposite page, far right: *1915 menu (© Joann Dost)***

together the best players from both sides of the bay and settle the question of supremacy between them. The eight players from the Claremont Country Club will deserve great credit if they can beat the best eight players from the San Francisco and Presidio golf clubs.

In 1912 invitations were sent out for ten-pin and quintet bowling tournaments. A domino tournament was *open to all male members* and had an entry fee of fifty cents, and trap and skeet shooting events also were held. The skeets were fashioned out of slate that was found on the golf course, and they were called *blue rocks* because of their predominate blue color. They were sold for one cent each, and a box of twenty-five shotgun shells cost seventy-five cents. Exactly where this activity took place is unknown, and the 1913 annual report indicated member interest in trap shooting had declined.

Dances were held most Saturday evenings in the ballroom, and these large get-togethers were sometimes preceded by smaller parties at members' homes, the details of which were frequently reported in local society columns. The dances often featured a live band, and occasionally a dance would be organized at the last minute to celebrate a special event. Providing live music on short notice was not always possible, so in 1913 the Club approved the purchase of new dance records for the Victrola, which

UPON New Year's Eve the customary Club Dinner will be omitted although meals will be served to those desiring it, provided previous notice is given.

A Special Supper will be served promptly at 10:30 p. m. at one dollar and a half per plate, and members are requested to reserve tables as early as possible.

Cancellations will not be allowed after noon on Dec. 31, 1916, unless the table can be given to another party.

The usual charge of one dollar for guests will be made.

A carefully chosen orchestra will play during supper and for dancing in the evening. Dancing will commence at midnight and continue till two a. m.

**Please read the enclosed cards carefully.**

HOUSE COMMITTEE.

was considered to be *very satisfactory for impromptu dances.*

When America entered World War I, many members of Claremont Country Club were personally affected. They rallied to help organizations such as the Red Cross by sponsoring tournaments for war relief. In addition to the war, Claremont also was affected by a different type of national crisis—the great influenza epidemic of 1918. Although records do not indicate how long the Club was closed, local, state, and federal mandates against people gathering together in order to prevent the spread of infectious disease required suspension of Club activities for some time.

When the war ended, parties were held for returning servicemen and for those who had helped on the home front. These were dry parties, because Prohibition had been enacted in 1919. Most members had access to their own private stock, but information about these indiscretions was kept within each household. Since Prohibition was very unpopular, many people correctly thought it was just a matter of time before it was repealed.

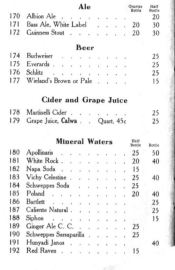

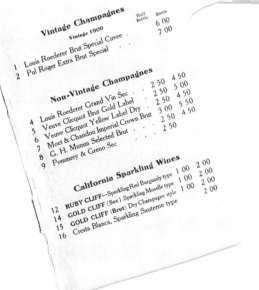

A notice was discreetly printed on the back of a program for the Club's 1919–20 New Year's Eve celebration that read, *In the event of Prohibition being lifted on or before New Year's Eve, a Special Wine List will be mailed to those reserving tables.* While the members were correct about the repeal of Prohibition, their timing was off by more than a decade.

So much has been made of the exciting era known as the Roaring '20s that one would expect Claremont's archives would yield colorful materials on this period. Sadly, and perhaps because of the subsequent clubhouse fire, no photographs or written accounts from that period have been found. One can only imagine the clubhouse atmosphere with flapper-dressed women dancing the Charleston.

Right: *The W. A. Barbour Annual Handicap Championship Trophy (© Joann Dost)*

Opposite page, clockwise from left:
*(1) Holiday Trophy, (2) Shooting Trophy,*
*(3) 1913 Labor Day Tournament Trophy,*
*(4) Home-and-Home Trophy from 1914 event*
*between Claremont and Presidio, and*
*(5) Walton N. Moore Trophy, circa 1920s.*
*The trophies shown are not to scale. (© Joann Dost)*

# FIRE RAZES CLAREMONT CLUB; GUESTS LOSE $20,000 JEWELS

## "PEACHES" MOBBED AT TRIAL

**How Flames Destroyed Noted Club**

MORE THAN a dozen pieces of fire fighting apparatus responded to the call from the blazing Claremont Country club, and the cameramen caught five of the fire fighters directing a stream of water in vain against the leaping flames.
—Post-Enquirer photo.

AS THE WALLS FELL, the flames leaped higher and higher, until only the steel posts remained standing. Photo shows the heart of the Claremont Country club after the blaze starting in the night had practically destroyed the structure.

AFTER THE FLAMES died down beneath a deluge of water, it was discovered that one man was missing. Later a badly burned body was found in the ruins of one of the fiercest fires Oakland has seen in a long time.

RUINED WALLS today mark what was the society center of the East Bay. Flying sparks from the wind-fanned flames threatened other buildings for many blocks, but the firemen succeeded in saving them. Fire Chief Sam Short directed the battle against the flames.

**AGED MAN PERISHES FIGHTING**

**Club Official Tells Escape From Fire; Rescue**

B.W. Bailey, general manager of Post-Inter-Ray, secretary of the Claremont Country club, and trustee of the club, escape of his wife and friend from...

## THE POST ENQUIRER

OAKLAND

Oakland—World City Beautiful

Industrial Capital of the West

OAKLAND, CALIFORNIA. MONDAY, JANUARY 24, 1927

The Post-Enquirer First Greatest 1871

Vol. 6. No. 20—The Post Enquirer

**FINAL HOME 2¢ AROUND BAY ELSEWHERE 5¢**

TWO CENTS

CHAPLIN PLANS RETURN

42

# THE FIRE AND REBUILDING
## THE CLUBHOUSE

Early in the morning of January 24, 1927, tragedy struck the thriving Claremont Country Club, when a four-alarm fire completely destroyed the clubhouse. By dawn all that remained were three tall chimneys above the smoking ruins. Fortunately, there were few guests in the clubhouse that night.

All of the occupants were asleep when the fire broke out. B. W. Railey, the Club's secretary and a future Club president, and his wife stayed at the Club that evening. According to the January 24, 1927, edition of *The Oakland Post Enquirer*, Railey said,

*We were awakened by what we thought was an explosion, to find our room was filled with smoke . . . We started for the stairway, but were turned back by walls of smoke and flame. Our only other means of escape was a window, and from this I managed to lower Mrs. Railey, by using blankets from the bed, to . . . the sun porch below.*

## CHAPTER 3

RUINS OF CLAREMONT COUNTRY CLUBHOUSE — One man was burned to death and nine persons were saved from a similar fate when fire destroyed the fashionable Claremont Country clubhouse at Broadway and Clifton street. The damage was estimated at more than $250,000 by B. W. Railey, the club secretary. The fire is believed to have originated in waste oil in the furnace room and was discovered by one of the club directors. This picture is a general view of the ruins.                    (P & A Photo)

*The devastating fire at Claremont Country Club caused the death of Charles Waterman, the Club's watchman.*

Facing page: *Newspaper photographs show the fire at Claremont Country Club completely destroyed the clubhouse and its contents. (© Joann Dost)*

43

Luigi "Louis" Galletti, Claremont's greenskeeper for forty-eight years, lived nearby and watched the fire devour the clubhouse. His son, Aldo, remembered his father looking out the living room window from their home near College Avenue and saying, *Jesus Cristo! The Club is on fire!*

Another witness to the fire was Mrs. Beatrice Badley, who was the daughter of the Club's manager, Edward A. Watson. She was eleven years old at that time and stated,

*It was about 3 A.M. when father heard scratching or knocking on the screened window of his bedroom. It was Charles Waterman, the night watchman who informed him that the Club was on fire. He told Watson he was going back to alert guests and try to save some valuable trophies. Watson told him to forget about the trophies, it was too dangerous. I was watching from the window, and at first there was no major blaze visible. But soon flames shot up from the backside of the clubhouse and just kept getting worse. When the Club was fully engulfed, I remember vividly that the four-stories-high-tall cupola started to lean to the left and then just tipped over and crashed into the blazing lower floors. The fire spread easily, because there were gaps between walls and because the fireman had little hydrant pressure for their hoses. The next morning there was nothing standing except the three stone chimneys. Mr. Waterman perished in the fire. The housekeeper was also missing; however, it was later learned that she slept away at a friend's house that night, something she rarely did. The office of the Club was to the left of the main entrance, and there was a trophy area to the right. The firemen continued to spray water on the large safe in the office to keep it cool to preserve its contents.*

After the fire, when rebuilding was authorized, Badley remembered her father went to San Francisco on many occasions to meet with the architect, George Kelham. She also remembered he took a trip to the East to make major purchases of new Club furniture, and the minutes show that Watson was authorized to travel with Director Bert Railey for this purpose. Watson had come to Claremont from Arizona and was hired by Robert Fitzgerald, whom Badley much admired. In 1931 Watson became ill with a severe form of tonsillitis, and he was told by his physician to take six months off and try to recover. Watson did not work after that. Badley's mother played a major role in the design and decoration of the new manager's cottage, which was built to match the new clubhouse. It replaced the small cottage that Badley had grown up in on the same site.

Facing page: *Louis Galletti (right), Claremont's greens-keeper for forty-eight years, witnessed the fire firsthand from his house near College Avenue. Galletti is shown with his son, Aldo, who learned to play golf at Claremont. In addition to winning many local tournaments, Aldo won the NCGA Junior Championship in 1937.*

In a heroic effort to save the lives of others, the Club's watchman became trapped and was killed by the flames. He was the only fatality. The *Post Enquirer* wrote,

> *The body of Charles Waterman, burned beyond recognition, was found by police and firemen in the heart of the ruins shortly after daybreak. By the side of the unrecognizable torso lay a fire extinguisher, mute evidence of the fight the aged man had put up to save not only other lives, but the building as well.*

Mrs. B. W. Railey described Waterman:

> *A faithful old fellow . . . the last I saw of him he was running in and out of the building, awakening servants and guests. He undoubtedly gave his life to save others in the burning building. From what I could gather, Waterman lost his life when he rushed into the building to save Miss Schimonek, the housekeeper.*

Others in the fire escaped with little more than their nightclothes. Many were permanent residents at the Club who lost all their worldly possessions. Mrs. Railey had put twenty thousand dollars worth of jewelry in a case that was later found empty, apparently stripped by one of the thousands of spectators said to have witnessed the blaze. She was able to save some silver fox furs by tossing them out an upper-floor window, and the furs were just about the only valuables saved from the fire.

The cause of the fire is still unclear, but the fire appeared to have started in waste oil in the furnace room. The clubhouse and everything in it were completely destroyed. Included in the devastation were most of the Club's records, approximately fifty thousand dollars worth of furnishings, and a variety of trophies and pieces of art that were considered priceless. Recently, two major trophies from the 1920s that were thought to be lost in the fire were located and were returned to the trophy case: the Walton N. Moore and the W. A. Barbour golf trophies. More importantly, the minutes of Board of Directors' meetings from January 1903 to January 1905 have been discovered. Thus, it appears that Waterman was able to save some of Claremont's early history before he died in the fire. Although damages from the fire were estimated at two hundred fifty thousand dollars, the clubhouse and its fixtures were only insured for two hundred twenty-five thousand dollars.

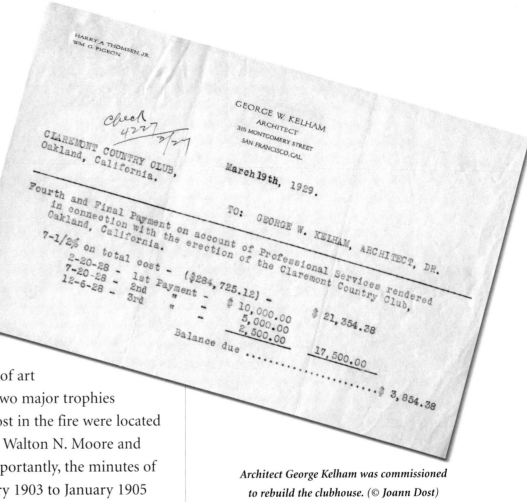

*Architect George Kelham was commissioned to rebuild the clubhouse. (© Joann Dost)*

The main lounge in the new Claremont Country Club, Oakland, is finished in California Redwood which has been specially treated with an antique stain effect and protected by clear lacquer, bringing out the full natural beauty of the wood.

George W. Kelham, Architect Taylor and Jackson, Builders A. Quandt & Sons, Painters and Decorators (since 1885) 374 Guerrero Street, San Francisco, California

By the day after the fire, the *Oakland Tribune* reported the determination of Claremont's leaders to remain and rebuild. *Although no conferences have been held yet, I believe plans for rebuilding a club-house on a larger more modern scale will be started immediately,* said Edward A. Watson, manager of the Club. The golf course had not been damaged, and the caddie house was still intact. The Club's Board of Directors began to work on the design and the financial details of a new structure. The members were asked in a November 1, 1927, questionnaire for their approval to increase the indebtedness of the Club to not more than two hundred sixty-five thousand dollars. A month later the Board sent a letter to the membership that stated, *In answer to the question-naire sent to the members on November 1, 1927 asking for their assent or dissent to increase the indebtedness of the club during 1928 for the building and refurbishing of a new clubhouse, the same was approved by a vote of 309 in favor and 25 against, 109 did not answer or were absent.* The letter also noted that some of the money would be allocated for Robert Hunter to begin reconstruction of the greens on the 2nd, 3rd, and 12th holes. Hunter was the construction partner of noted golf course architect

Alister MacKenzie, who had redesigned much of the course in late 1925 and 1926.

During their meeting on January 27, 1928, the Board of Directors unanimously agreed to begin taking steps to rebuild the clubhouse on the original site. The Board cited the importance of the Club's social activities in the past and the desire to have the clubhouse available for such affairs in the near future. George W. Kelham, a prominent architect, then approached the Board with a set of clubhouse plans he had prepared for the Burlingame Golf Club. Burlingame had decided to occupy the former Crocker mansion in Hillsborough and no longer needed the plans. The grand Tudor design and the size of the plans were considered a perfect fit for both the style the Board sought and the site's location, so the Board accepted Kelham's proposed plans without delay. Having a completed set of plans in hand no doubt saved a year or more in constructing a new building. The construction firm of Charles L. Taylor and William Jackson was selected to build the new structure; the firm's bid for construction was approximately two hundred thirty-nine thousand dollars. At the same time, the Board appropriated an additional fifty thousand dollars for new furnishings.

The members continued to play golf without much interruption. The undamaged caddie house was still available, and in the interim, the stables, which had been built in 1891, were remodeled with lockers, showers, and lounge facilities. After the new club-

Facing page: *Construction of Claremont's new clubhouse took approximately two years.*

house was built, this structure was converted into a three-story employees' dormitory, which was demolished in 1976.

Two years after the fire, the new clubhouse was formally opened on Saturday evening, February 9, 1929. The event was covered in the February 10, 1929, edition of the *Oakland Tribune*.

*The new $350,000 home of the Claremont Country Club, at Broadway and Clifton, was thrown open to its members and guests yesterday.*

The greater cost reported by the newspaper was about right when the building, furnishings, and landscaping were finally tallied.

*Nearly 500 persons visited the club home between 3 and 5 o'clock. English Tudor type with brown stucco, English gabled roof, two stories in front, three in rear. The entire lower floor of the building is given over to the men members. The men's quarters open on a brick terrace overlooking the putting green, now near completion. The architects have provided plenty of locker space and showers. Adjoining the main locker rooms are quarters for the junior members of the club. The club is provided with a large grill, finished in dark wood and furnishings, where golfers may have luncheon at their leisure. The lower floor includes a buffet and smoking room.*

*The entrance hall of the club is one of its most attractive features. It is designed in the early Tudor period, and a massive mantel and fireplace add to its charm. A grand staircase leads from the main floor to the second floor, which is given over to suites for club members and their guests. These upper rooms are finished in ivory, and furnished to the taste of the individual occupant. Soft tones prevail in the main lounge on the first floor. The rug in the lounge is copper-toned chenille, with window drapes to harmonize. Lamps, davenports and occasional chairs are in soft greens, tans and blues. The cathedral ceiling is of beamed redwood, trimmed in walnut, with Gothic arches. A long sunroom, provided with wicker furniture, overlooks the golf course. A large tea-room is provided in the north wing exclusively for women members. This is finished in the softer shades of Wilton velvet rugs and drapes.*

Claremont Country Club had survived its darkest hour.

# THE GREAT DEPRESSION
# AND WAR YEARS

The opening of Claremont's beautiful new clubhouse was a happy occasion. Unfortunately, there were less joyful times ahead. During the next two decades, Claremont Country Club faced the hardships of the Great Depression and World War II. Many members fell on hard financial times and could not pay their Club bills. They were allowed to resign and to transfer their memberships to approved applicants who were willing to pay the past due balances plus the transfer fees. The Club survived and did better than the other clubs in the area, some of which were forced to close. Perhaps the greatest annoyance to many members was Prohibition, which was in effect from 1920 until its repeal in 1933. During that time the members did not hold major activities with the same enthusiasm as before Prohibition.

Facing page and above: *After the repeal of Prohibition and before the start of World War II, Claremont members were eager to resume social festivities.* (© *Joann Dost*)

The year 1932 brought forth a very fortunate development in the Club's history. For years Claremont's members had been disturbed by the noise, vibrations, and occasional dangers of flying rocks that came from the blasting operations at Bilger Rock Quarry, which was located between the 10th fairway and Pleasant Valley Road, until the firm finally fell victim to the Great Depression and closed its operations. Thanks to the foresight of Charles A. Beardsley, a member who posted the option money, Claremont bought the quarry property on November 14, 1932, for fifteen thousand dollars. The quarry acquisition benefited Claremont in a couple of important ways: there was permanent abatement of the

*Charles Jackson and Horatio Harper playing dominos, circa 1930s. Dominos is still a highly competitive game at Claremont. (© Joann Dost)*

CLAREMONT COUNTRY CLUB
OAKLAND, CALIFORNIA

Domino Tournament begins February the first—open to all male members—flights of sixteen—when signed—names to be put in hat and entered on sheet as drawn and thereafter play match play—winner of two or three consecutive games to "Go Up"—finals in each flight to play for Club Championship and prizes as determined by the Committee.

You can enter every flight and not more than five times in each flight—each entry 50c to be put on your monthly card.

Rules governing play posted in the lounging room.

DOMINO TOURNAMENT COMMITTEE

many nuisances, and for an additional eighty-five hundred dollars, the quarry was converted into the present-day reservoir that has given Claremont an abundant, low-cost source of water for seventy years. It is calculated that the quarry's water capacity when full, is sufficient for at least two years of course irrigation in case of drought.

*Other competitive events included this putting contest, which was held during the 1930s.*

*An early-day activity that was discontinued after the 1950s was lawn bowling.*

With the start of World War II, there were many changes to Club activities, some of which were permanent. Several Club members and employees left the comforts of Claremont to serve their country, and, as a result, the Club had difficulty finding competent help. Claremont members continued to dine at the Club on Thursdays and Sundays—"maids' nights out"—until October 1942, when the Board suspended non-member dinners and parties on those nights because of a lack of staff.

The annual Christmas party was cancelled in 1942, 1943, and 1944 because many members felt it was inappropriate to have holiday parties when so many men and women were serving their country overseas. Members assisted with mowing and the general upkeep of the golf course during this period, and some even chose not to play golf in deference to those serving in the war.

In April 1942 the Board agreed to discontinue the purchase of fresh fruits and vegetables from its San Francisco suppliers because of gasoline rationing and the increased cost

for delivery. Also during the war, the Club's staff was reminded that it was illegal to serve liquor to men in uniform before 5:00 P.M. or after midnight. By 1943 a total of twenty-seven members were serving in the military, and while they were serving in the war, their dues were forgiven. The Board also granted special privileges to many military officers who were stationed in the area.

Quality distilled spirits were becoming difficult to obtain, and the Club's inventories began to shrink. In 1943 the Board recognized there was potential for disaster, so it found a source for a large, one-time purchase of eighty-five hundred dollars worth of liquor, which certainly kept the members' spirits high.

During this period many of the early sporting activities, including skeet and archery, were abandoned; however, the members' interest in lawn bowling returned. In the fall of 1940, a bowling green was installed in the area that is now occupied by tennis courts seven and eight. The green was dedicated on October 18, 1940, when a fundraising event to benefit the Allied Relief Fund was held and teams from Berkeley, Lakeside, and Oakland competed with the Claremont bowlers. Eventually, lawn bowling once again fell by the wayside, and the smooth bowling surface was converted to a chipping green.

As the war years continued, life in the United States changed as food, clothing, and gasoline were rationed.

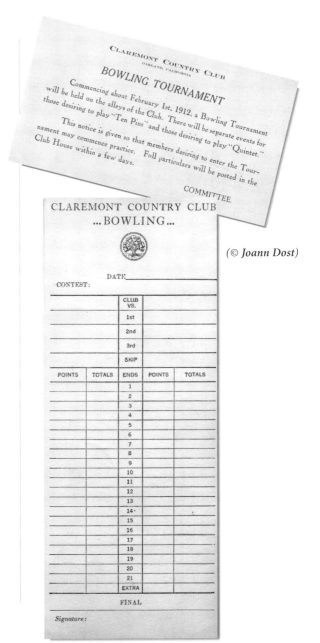

*(© Joann Dost)*

## NOSTALGIA...THE WARRIORS

Golfers serving Uncle Sam these days can come up with the most unique yarns in eagerness for the sport in their off-time.

Take Jack Selby of Oakland. He's a Navy lieutenant who pilots transports out into the Pacific.

On recent runs Selby has been stopping for a short while at Hawaii both going and coming. The isle is the scene of an interesting golf tale.

A month or so ago upon landing in Hawaii Selby bumped into—of all people—an old Oakland golfing buddy, Bud Ehmann, who is now Lieut. Comdr. George C. Ehmann, working with the air transport service there.

At the time Ehmann, over a few lime cokes, we'd guess, mentioned to Selby the fine links on the island and that he had been playing lately with Johnny Perreleli, who you can recall was pro at the Lake Tahoe nine-hole layout before the war. Perrelli is an Army sergeant stationed on the isle.

But during the course of conversation Ehmann mentioned he wasn't doing so well with what clubs were available. He yearned for his own set.

Several weeks later Selby landed at the isle again. And saw Ehmann again. The latter almost did a nose dive when he saw what was hung over Jack's right shoulder—Bud's golf bag chock full of sticks.

Naturally that called for a match.

**Lieut. Comdr. Ehmann**

enant was an odd sight as he leaped out of his transport with brief case under arm and a golf bag over his shoulder. Like a Summer tourist landing on the Palm-treed isle. But it was early Spring and in an off-time during a war.

The next a.m. Selby and Ehmann took to the Waialai Country Club course. It was like old times back in Oakland. A great time was had by all. Ehmann fashioned a 74 to beat Selby.

Now that he has his own clubs Ehmann is getting as much enjoyment on the links as possible, relates Selby. He also reports that Perrelli is in rare form, shooting in the high 60s.

While in Oakland Selby has been enjoying himself playing with another old buddy, Hy Hennings of Piedmont, who recently was commissioned an ensin and is waiting overseas duty. They played at the Claremont Country Club the other day with Selby scoring a 70, two-over-par, and Hennings 71. That's darn good for a couple of guys who have been busy in the service.

Louie Galletti, veteran greens-keeper at Claremont, relates his son Aldo, one of the best local tournament players before going into the Army, is out of the hospital in England and back on the continent.

Aldo wrote his parents that before leaving the British Isles he was able to play several times. He mailed a score card here which showed h' had a 38 for nine holes. It was fou over par.

But Selby didn't have his clubs this time. So a duel was slated for Jack's next arrival. It was just a week or so ago that Selby again flew out of the Pacific and on to Hawaii.

It was late at night and the lieut-

Above: *This newspaper article describes an interesting meeting during World War II between two of Claremont's members, Jack Selby and Bud Ehmann.*

Right: *The use of the terrace has always been popular at Claremont.*

Opposite page: *Christmas party, 1941 (© Joann Dost)*

Claremont was already experiencing labor shortages, so in March 1944 the Board of Directors decided to close the Club on Mondays. This gave the limited number of available employees a much-needed day of rest, and it is a practice that continues today. Initially, this day off applied to the clubhouse only; it was not until the early 1960s that the closure was extended to the golf course as well.

Even after the war, shortages continued. According to the minutes of the October 15, 1947, Board of Directors' meeting, *The Board requested that manager Henry Ploennis comply with President Truman's request for meatless Tuesdays and eggless and poultryless Thursdays.* Claremont's chef must have created some interesting meals.

*"Mom" Traynor and Felix Mehan*

*Fred Greenlee, Bill Oliver, and John Rosson*

Facing page: *Trophy case with grill in background*

The interior of the clubhouse had remained virtually un-
changed since the building was reconstructed in 1928 and 1929.
With the growing economic prosperity that followed the end of the
war, many members wanted to renovate and upgrade Claremont's
facilities to reflect the modern times. Deciding what the new look
should be, or even if there should be a change at all, became a
matter of dispute. The Board of Directors held an open meeting on
November 30, 1948, to discuss a proposed plan for remodeling the
main lounge. The plan included *lowering the ceiling, remodeling the
fireplace, putting in four plate glass windows and the acquisition of
new furniture, lamps, floor coverings, etc.* According to the minutes
from that meeting, one member felt *he represented the "loyal opposition" and claimed that the group he represented felt that the style
of redecoration already accomplished in the dining room, lobby, and
porch was unsuitable. He felt that the main lounge should not be
changed.* He was referring to the redwood and walnut woodwork

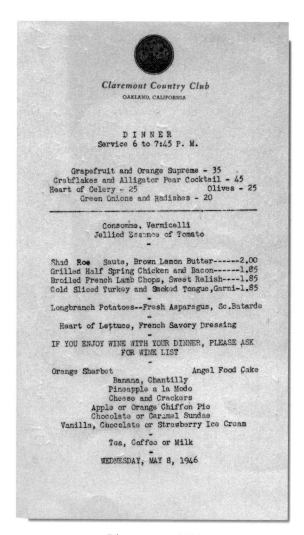

*Dinner menu, 1946*

that had been covered with white paint, light wall coverings, and softer-toned carpeting, which was a radical change from the former Tudor look.

Because of this strong opposition, the remodeling was not completed for six years. In 1954 the clear-heart redwood beams, columns, panels, moldings, and millwork in the stately clubhouse were painted, and the vaulted ceiling in the lounge was hidden by a false ceiling made of acoustical tile. Even after the changes were in place, some members did not approve of the new, modern appearance. By 1967 the lounge ceiling was restored to its original height, but the details of the beautiful redwood and its perfect grain are still covered in layers of paint.

Other changes were to follow, the most significant of which occurred in 1979, when the members approved a cocktail lounge next to the main lounge that displaced the club manager's office. It is seldom that changes are met with total membership approval, but everyone agrees Claremont has been well maintained, and the members take pride in its continuing beauty.

While changes to the Club's interior caused quite a stir, changes to the exterior also caused controversy. Although the issue of a swimming pool was first discussed during a Board meeting in August 1936, the actual construction of such a facility was repeatedly tabled by the Board until 1949, when the construction of a Club swimming pool was discussed again. There was spirited debate among the members, and some members resigned or threatened to resign over an addition to what they felt should remain a golf club. Certainly it was the intention of Claremont's founders, as was expressly stated and borne out by the activities of the Club's early members, to encourage practice of all healthy outdoor sports.

The burden of these conflicting viewpoints fell on E. P. Crossan, Claremont's seventeenth president (1948–50). He and his Board finally faced the issue when they put to the membership their proposal to borrow fifty thousand dollars for the construction of a pool, which was approved by a vote of 301 to 66 in December 1949. Club member Clarence Mayhew was the architect of the pool and its adjoining structures, which were both built and opened in 1950. The pool has been an asset to the Club ever since.

### BENEFITS OF THE QUARRY PURCHASE

In 1966 Claremont Country Club President Thomas Ashby and his successor, Eugene Sweetland, represented the Club in negotiations with the developers of a shopping center that was to be built adjacent to the quarry/reservoir. In exchange for allowing the developers to put some fill in the west end of the quarry, the developers raised the outlet of the reservoir and its pump house. This work was done without cost to the Club, and it increased the capacity of the reservoir to approximately 35 million gallons.

For a brief period during the 1960s, the reservoir also served as home port of the "Claremont Navy." The fleet consisted of a blunt-end duck boat that was about eight feet long and was used to retrieve floating golf balls. In the absence of a regular practice range, the reservoir served that purpose. Golf pro Tal Smith purchased a supply of floating golf balls, and a practice tee was installed at the north end of the reservoir. Once a week the "naval crew," which consisted of Smith and John Fite, retrieved the floating balls with a fish net. Alas, the venture was short-lived, and the "Claremont Navy" was soon retired. Theft of the floating practice balls was an annoyance; however, the real problem was that the balls, which presented an attractive nuisance to youngsters, were too difficult to safely retrieve by the staff. The idea was not completely void of merit, but the potential for disaster was just too great.

Another benefit of the 1932 quarry acquisition was the land it provided for a new 10th hole. The 10th tee was once located below the 18th green and next to the tennis courts. Its small green was a cut into the hillside below and forward of the 11th tee. A player had to either loft a very accurate shot or hit directly into the steep bank above the 10th green and then hope the ball would roll back onto it. Either way, it was not a satisfactory golf hole. Completed in the mid-1930s, today's 10th hole is about thirty yards west of the old hole.

The quarry purchase also included some property that was located above the reservoir on Montgomery Street, which was sold by the Club in 1981 for one hundred fifty thousand dollars. This was considerably more than the original purchase price of fifteen thousand dollars. An additional benefit to selling the land was the substantial reduction in the Club's liability risk for intruders who fell into the reservoir. Claremont still owns and leases the land between the reservoir and Pleasant Valley Avenue, which is now occupied by a restaurant.

## THE OAK TREE FUND

This fund was established in January 1979 at the suggestion of Dr. Albert Rowe, who served as its first Chairman, and its purpose is to provide a means for Club members to contribute to the improvement of clubhouse facilities, to the beautification of both the grounds and the golf course, and to the financial assistance for employees with special needs. The Club's normal operating expenses and routine maintenance are excluded from consideration, and donations to the fund may be designated for a specific purpose. Monetary gifts are accepted, and some donations have been made in memory of Club members. Requests are granted by the Board of Directors and the Oak Tree Committee, which manages the fund. The fund has covered the cost of special plantings on both the golf course and the grounds, including ornamental memorial trees. Decorative clubhouse items also have been provided, including planters, frames for paintings and historic documents, and trophy cases to house memorabilia.

### THE DIAMOND JUBILEE

Claremont Country Club celebrated its seventy-fifth anniversary in 1979. The event commemorated the Club's 1904 opening at its present-day location; however, this was actually the seventy-sixth year of Claremont's 1903 incorporation. It also was the eighty-second year since the original Oakland Golf Club was founded in 1897. Perhaps future generations will correct both of these anomalies and celebrate the bicentennial in 2097.

Under the leadership of Club President Lee Emerson (1979–80), several innovative activities were started. For example, in February 1979 the first issue of *Claremont Country Club News* was published. Credit for the inception and the continuing success of this publication belongs to

*Eugene Sweetland, who was President of Claremont in 1967–68, is shown with a time capsule that was one of the Diamond Jubilee's many activities.*

*Opposite page: Concert on the Green*

many Club members, particularly Dollie Shaw and Arthur Crist. The monthly newsletter remains an interesting, informative journal that addresses the Club's history as well as its current activities.

In August 1979 Claremont created Concert on the Green, an event for its Seventy-Fifth Anniversary, and it remains a much-anticipated annual event. The Claremont Men's Chorus, which was started by former assistant tennis professional Bob Hammerlee, is still the main feature of Concert on the Green. Maryly Johnson is the chorus' loyal and gifted accompanist.

At the beginning of 1979, Emerson appointed Tom Martz the Jubilee's chairman. Martz' talent for showmanship helped develop many fun events that year, which ended with the formal Diamond Jubilee Dinner Dance.

# CLAREMONT
# AT THE CLOSE OF THE CENTURY

## CHAPTER 6

### FLAGS AND FIRES

From the earliest days of Claremont Country Club, the American flag has been prominently displayed in front of the Club. In 1990 the Club needed to replace its largest flagpole because of dry rot. This immense pole was one hundred feet tall and was visible around the Bay Area from as far away as Berkeley and the Bay Bridge. The pole was installed at Claremont after it was purchased during the close of the 1939 World's Fair at Treasure Island. After considerable discussion about a replacement and its cost, a novel plan was approved by the Board.

The plan was devised by an eight-member committee that was chaired by John J. Donovan Jr., and two of the Club's members, Stefan Medwadowski and Arthur Nielsen, headed the engineering and the construction of the project. The plan called for the procurement of a new one-hundred-foot pole that would be installed in a brick patio in the garden next to the club manager's residence. The projected cost was thirty thousand dollars, and funds were

*Facing page: Tournament flags are flown from the clubhouse. (© Joann Dost)*

*Claremont has proudly flown the
American flag since the Club's inception.*

Opposite page: *Fire above 15th green as viewed from
Village Market, October 20, 1991*

raised by private donations. Members or relatives who wished to memorialize a deceased member with a one-thousand-dollar donation could have that person's name added to a bronze memorial plaque. Forty-five people subscribed to this level, and they have had names added to the plaque that sits atop a brick pedestal next to the new pole. The new one-hundred-foot pole, which was turned on a special lathe in Bellevue, Washington, was installed on a twelve-foot foundation in December 1990. All excess funds were turned over to the Oak Tree Committee.

### FIRESTORM

The morning of October 20, 1991, began as a hot autumn day with strong gusty winds in the hills of Oakland and Berkeley. Those winds rekindled the embers of a small fire from the previous day in the Claremont Hills area, and the embers became a fire that spread furiously south toward the Montclair and Rockridge Districts of Oakland. The heat and the winds were so intense that the inferno jumped the eight lanes of Highway 24 below the Caldecott Tunnel, and the air was so hot that homes literally exploded and automobile engines melted into pools of metal. By the end of the day, the firestorm had destroyed nearly thirty-four hundred homes and apartments and had claimed the lives of twenty-five people. It was the nation's worst urban fire—there was loss of life and property that had not been seen since the great San Francisco earthquake and fire in 1906.

Although the clubhouse was never threatened, Claremont Country Club was still affected by the firestorm in numerous ways. At least twenty-three members and one employee lost their homes to the flames, and some of those members sought refuge at the Club for rest, meals, and available rooms until they could find suitable shelter. Damage to Claremont was limited to parts of the golf course—the fire swept through nine acres of undeveloped Club property along Broadway Terrace by the 15th green, which was damaged, and there was extensive damage along

the 12th fairway, where the fire swept through the trees and the shrubbery between the golf course and the cemetery. The worst damage was done to the 12th green, the rail behind the 13th tee was burned, a cypress tree on the 13th hole was ignited by embers, there was damage along the service road by the 9th hole and on the 11th green, and the entire course was covered with ash and embers. Three trees near the 15th green along Clarewood Drive were cut down to help stop the spread of flames. That afternoon

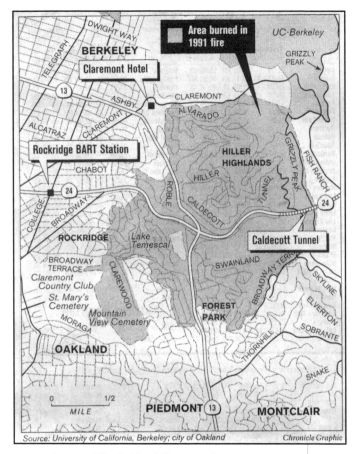

*A map of the Oakland firestorm that tore through the hills on October 20, 1991, shows Claremont was singed but was otherwise intact.*

Opposite page: *All-American lunch specials*

Opposite page, far right: *Claremont ushered in the new millennium with style.*

some of the Club's golf staff, members, and caddies pitched in to protect the area by monitoring the fire's progress and by setting up sprinklers. The Club's President, Grant Powell (1991–92), authorized the staff to open the Club dining room in order to serve meals to the members, employees, and caddies who had spent most of the day trying to protect the Club and its grounds from the fire. The clubhouse, which was secure, served as a brief safe haven for neighbors who lost their homes. Unfortunately, the natural gas supply was cut off for five days, which meant there was no heat, hot water, or hot meals.

## THE SECOND MILLENNIUM

As the 1990s came to a close, Claremont Country Club planned to celebrate the end of the twentieth century with a masked Millennium Ball. It cost two hundred dollars per person, which was twice as much as a full Club membership cost in 1903. At that time there were people predicting doom in the form of world famine, computer crashes, cash shortages, and other dire consequences, but Claremont's ball went on in spite of that with marvelous food, music, and celebrations. After midnight arrived, dancing and singing continued well into the early morning. When members rose later in the day, they found the world was still functioning, and everyone breathed a little easier.

Millennium
Venetian
Ball

Claremont Country Club
welcomes you to the
"Millennium Venetian Ball"
Dance the night away
and welcome the new century!
Friday, December 31, 1999
Cocktails 8:00 Dinner 9:00
Black tie

Less than two years later on September 11, 2001, the West Coast awakened to news that the United States had been attacked by terrorists in both New York City and Washington, D.C. This event, which was considered to be worse than the attack on Pearl Harbor some sixty years earlier, shook the entire world. None of this directly affected Claremont, but a lot of the members felt the emotional impact. The attack created a renewal of patriotism, and Claremont responded in its own small way by introducing American-style "comfort food" on red, white, and blue menus.

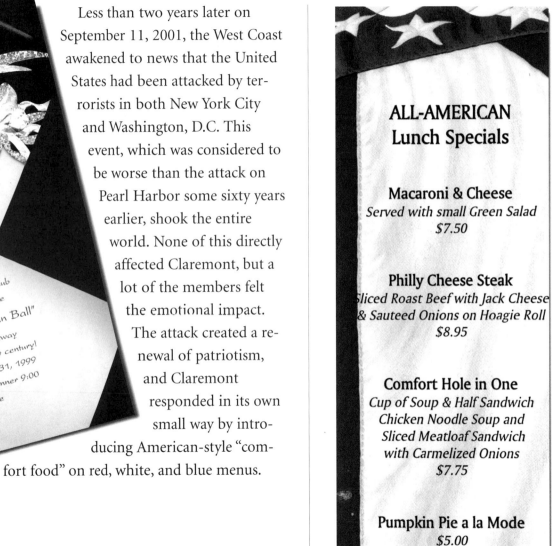

**ALL-AMERICAN Lunch Specials**

**Macaroni & Cheese**
*Served with small Green Salad*
*$7.50*

**Philly Cheese Steak**
*Sliced Roast Beef with Jack Cheese & Sauteed Onions on Hoagie Roll*
*$8.95*

**Comfort Hole in One**
*Cup of Soup & Half Sandwich Chicken Noodle Soup and Sliced Meatloaf Sandwich with Carmelized Onions*
*$7.75*

**Pumpkin Pie a la Mode**
*$5.00*

*Macdonald Smith's golf clubs (© Joann Dost)*

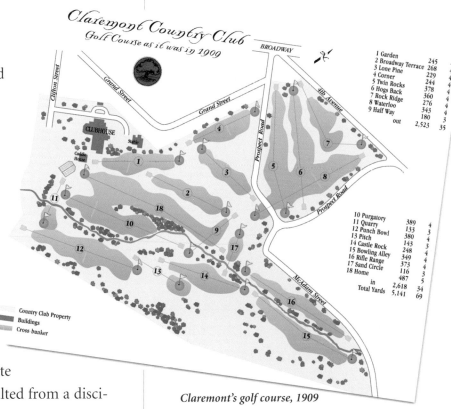

| 1 Garden | 245 | 4 |
| 2 Broadway Terrace | 268 | 4 |
| 3 Lone Pine | 229 | 4 |
| 4 Corner | 244 | 4 |
| 5 Twin Rocks | 378 | 4 |
| 6 Hogs Back | 360 | 4 |
| 7 Rock Ridge | 276 | 4 |
| 8 Waterloo | 343 | 4 |
| 9 Half Way | 180 | 3 |
| out | 2,523 | 35 |

| 10 Purgatory | 389 | 4 |
| 11 Quarry | 133 | 3 |
| 12 Punch Bowl | 380 | 4 |
| 13 Pitch | 143 | 3 |
| 14 Castle Rock | 248 | 4 |
| 15 Bowling Alley | 349 | 4 |
| 16 Rifle Range | 373 | 4 |
| 17 Sand Circle | 116 | 3 |
| 18 Home | 487 | 5 |
| in | 2,618 | 34 |
| Total Yards | 5,141 | 69 |

*Claremont's golf course, 1909*
*(© Eureka Cartography)*

## THE GOLF COURSE

Unlike many of the early courses that started with nine or fewer golf holes, Claremont Country Club opened in 1904 with eighteen holes. Official credit for the design of the original layout goes to James "Pop" Smith, patriarch of the famous golf family from Carnoustie, Scotland. As Claremont's first greenskeeper, Smith was most interested in how the course would be designed on the Club's 107 acres of land. The concept of golf architecture was barely known in the United States when Claremont was founded, and several more years would pass before it began to develop into the art it has become today. Hence, it is quite unlikely that the original golf course layout resulted from a disciplined design plan that is attributable to any one person. It most

likely involved as much input from George Smith, the Club's first golf professional, as it did from his father.

There have been some significant changes in the design of the golf course. In 1923 and 1924, the eucalyptus forest next to the cemetery was cleared, and a new 12th hole was constructed. This extended the course by nearly four hundred yards, which significantly rerouted the course. After the 1st and 2nd holes were combined into one long 1st hole, the front nine holes were shifted forward, which caused the finishing hole at the clubhouse to be renumbered the 9th hole instead of the 10th. With the new 12th hole, it was necessary to reverse the direction of play of the 13th from its former tee location to the left of the present-day 11th green, which was indeed an improvement.

Claremont's golf course was later remodeled by noted designer Alister MacKenzie, a Scot who was raised in England. MacKenzie gave up the practice of medicine and became an expert at military camouflage. After that experience, he devoted the rest of his life to golf course architecture.

MacKenzie came to the United States after World War 1, and remodeling Claremont's golf course was part of his early work in California. He planned the redesign during the fall of 1925, and it was implemented in 1927. This involved removing the fairway

*Left, inset: James "Pop" Smith was Claremont's first greenskeeper and designer of the original golf course.*

*Facing page: Claremont's golf course, circa 1915. Note the earthen berm hazards on the fairways and the original clubhouse toward the upper left. (© Joann Dost)*

*Below: The Smith family of golfers from Carnoustie, Scotland. Back row: Willie and Alec. Middle row: Mrs. Smith, George, and James Sr. Front row: James Jr. and Macdonald.*

cross-bunkers and adding intricate, strategically placed sand bunkers. The cross-bunkers, or mounded earth and grass berms, were designed as hazards that are similar to those in early-English steeplechase events. MacKenzie had enormous influence on the contemporary design of golf courses worldwide during the 1920s and early 1930s. In this country he is probably best known for the designs of Augusta National Golf Club and Cypress Point Club at Pebble Beach. Locally, he also designed the Meadow Club, Green Hills, Northwood, and Pasatiempo, where he lived and died in 1934.

The original eighteen holes at Claremont totaled 5,141 yards and were par 69. The remodeled golf course now totals 5,495 yards and is par 68. The increased yardage was the result of the changes to the 12th and 13th holes, and the reduction in par to 68 was the result of replacing the first three par-4 holes (total 12) with a par-5 1st hole and par-3 2nd and 3rd holes (total 11). All the original holes had names, some of which were changed to reflect the remodeled holes. During the mid-1970s, a capital-improvement expenditure was needed to replace the deteriorating irrigation system

*Alister MacKenzie (center, sitting) at Claremont in 1933. To his left is Donald Ross, another famed golf architect. (© Joann Dost)*

Top left: *The 12th fairway later became the 11th fairway, when the new 12th fairway was built in the upper right area of the photograph. (© Joann Dost)*

Bottom left: *View from the 14th stone tee and new clubhouse, 1929*

Facing page: *Alister MacKenzie*

and maintenance shed and to add fencing and cart paths. Don Dorward, Claremont's twenty-ninth President (1975–76), and the Board arranged five hundred fifty thousand dollars in capital funding. Although formal approval was not required by the bylaws, the members responded favorably to the Board's proposal to assess them for these improvements as well as the addition of two new tennis courts. During the mid-1990s, the drainage systems were further improved, and the irrigation systems were completely replaced with a highly sophisticated computerized sprinkler-control system that is operated from the golf course superintendent's office. The members approved yet another assessment to complete these improvements.

In September 2002 Claremont Country Club was certified by the prestigious Alister MacKenzie Society as its fourteenth member. The Society's membership consists of private golf clubs worldwide that are sponsored by a member club and that can provide proof that their courses were either designed or extensively redesigned by MacKenzie.

Founded in 1987 with the mission of researching and preserving MacKenzie's work, the Society also encourages programs to maintain the integrity of design and intent of the original MacKenzie golf courses. Its members include Cypress Point Club, Royal Melbourne, Lahinch, Valley Club, Pasatiempo, and Meadow Club. From Claremont's archives, and with the help of

Above: *3rd tee near Prospect (present-day Monroe) Avenue (© Joann Dost)*

Facing page: *16th green and "Rifle Range" fairway (© Joann Dost)*

*John Black*

retired golf professional John Fite, the Club's critical links with MacKenzie's work were established.

Claremont was sponsored by a past president of the Society and was invited to present its credentials as a legitimate Mac-Kenzie redesign. The Club's Board of Directors approved a plan to seek membership in the society and appointed Hal Lauth to lead the delegation and pursue the process. Ironically, Lauth was a guest at the Society's annual meeting at Crystal Downs in Michigan on September 11, 2001. Exactly one year later, a delegation led by Lauth, Club President Phil Sarkisian, Warren "Chip" Brown, Jay McDaniel, and Parry Wagener made the successful presentation during the Society's meeting at the Meadow Club.

### GOLF PROFESSIONALS

George Smith, son of greenskeeper James "Pop" Smith, was the first golf professional at the new Claremont Country Club. He served from 1904 to 1912; prior to that he had been manager of Oakland Golf Club.

John Lambie "Auld Jawn" Black was the next golf professional. Also a Scotsman, he succeeded Smith in 1913 and remained at Claremont for the next ten years before he left to join the California Golf Club. Black won the California Open three times, and in 1922 he tied for second in the U.S. Open at Skokie, Illinois with Bobby Jones. Gene Sarazan won the title that year in a three-way play off. Black was a great teacher of golf in the classic Scottish tradition. Eddie Redell, an old-time Claremont caddie, described him as a *tweedie sort of fellow,* and Black's trademark was a stem pipe clenched between his teeth. He had a sly sense of humor and was well liked. Black was inducted into the California Golf Hall of Fame in 1963; that year he passed away at the age of eighty-three.

In 1923 J. William Fries was appointed Claremont's golf professional, and he served when the new 12th hole was constructed and the course was rerouted. In 1927, the year of the disastrous clubhouse fire, Eliot Callender became Claremont's golf professional. He served for one year before he returned to his previous position as golf professional of Monterey Peninsula Country Club.

John Dewey Longworth arrived at Claremont in 1928, and he was the Club's golf professional until he retired in 1960. From 1934 to 1937, he also served as president of the Professional Golf Association's (PGA) Northern California Section. Longworth, who was known by his middle name, was elegant in both his manner and his dress, and he was an excellent instructor. Longworth also is credited with developing an outstanding junior golf program.

Above: *Dewey Longworth was Claremont's golf professional for thirty-two years.*

Left: *Dewey Longworth in Kansas City, 1926*

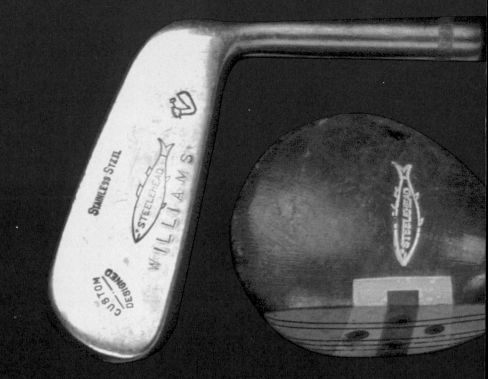

**Above:** *Howard Steele golf club (© Joann Dost)*

**Opposite page:** *Howard Steele is shown making customized golf clubs for Claremont's members.*

**Left:** *Dewey Longworth and ten-year-old Bobby Cristy, the first Junior golfer in the United States to receive a PGA diploma, October 1938*

During Longworth's tenure, the assistant golf professional, Howard Steele, made some of the members' golf clubs. He made woods and irons by assembling components such as heads and shafts, and grips were fitted to the individual. As a final touch, Steele stamped his trademark logo—Steelehead, which was surrounded by the outline of a fish—onto the clubheads.

Above: *Tal Smith (right) after he won the NCGA Open at Meadow Club in 1949. He beat Ken Venturi (left) 8 and 7. (© Joann Dost)*

Right: *Sports page cartoon by* Oakland Tribune *illustrator, Lee Susman, extolling the California State Open Championship win by Tal Smith in 1946.*

Opposite page, left: *Tal Smith Cup Trophy and Tal Smith's golf bag (© Joann Dost)*

Opposite page, top right: *Tal Smith (© Joann Dost)*

Opposite page, bottom right: *John Fite, Claremont's head golf professional from 1981 until 1999*

Talbert "Tal" Smith succeeded Longworth in 1961, and he was the head golf professional until he retired at the end of 1980. Smith was an accomplished aviator, including serving as an instructor for pilots of *P51 Mustangs* during World War II. He also was an intense competitor, and his first major golf victory was the California State Open Championship in 1946. Smith's golden moment was at the Fort Washington Golf Course in Fresno, where he set a new course record to win the state title by one stroke over Lloyd Mangrum, the U.S. Open champion that same year.

Smith won the Northern California Amateur Championship (match play) twice. He also won the Northern California Amateur Seventy-Two-Hole Championship (stroke play) four times. In addition, he won the Northern California PGA Stroke-Play Championship as an amateur in 1947 and as a professional in 1960, the Northern California PGA Match-Play Championship in 1964, and the Northern California PGA Seniors Tournament in 1977 and 1978. Smith was equally proud of winning the Alameda Commuters Tournament seven times. This Bay Area tournament was literally started by commuters on San Francisco Bay ferries seventy-five years ago, and it is still going strong today.

Smith was inducted into the California Golf Writers Hall of Fame in 1981, and in 1986 the Northern California Golf Association (NCGA) named him Grand Master, its most prestigious award. This tribute by an amateur golf association to a club professional is testament to Smith's character and his golfing ability. Claremont's annual Tal Smith Cup Tournament is a tribute to his popularity, and it features Highland dress, bagpipers, haggis, and perhaps a wee "drammie" to ward off the chill.

John Fite, Smith's assistant since 1964, succeeded Smith in 1981 as the head golf professional, and he served until he retired in 1999. Fite is known as an excellent instructor of the short game and the art of putting. A unique moment in his career was when he was invited to Russia to establish a junior golf team. He later took that team to Japan to play against other juniors in international competition.

After a national search for a new golf professional, the Selection Committee chose Jay McDaniel, who started in May 1999. His prior

professional experience was at Lake Merced Golf and Country Club; before that he was with Brookside Golf Club. Prior to those positions, he was the assistant professional at Pacific Grove Golf Links, the Links at Spanish Bay, and Chartwell Golf Club in Severna Park, Maryland. McDaniel has brought new energy to the golf program and has introduced innovative teaching techniques. His wife, Nancy, who leads summer clinics at the Club, is the first women's golf coach at the University of California, Berkeley.

## COURSE SUPERINTENDENTS

Claremont's golf course superintendents, who used to be called head greenskeepers, have played a vital role in the Club's success. The first was James "Pop" Smith, the principal designer of the course. John Neville was the next superintendent; Louis Galletti followed Neville and served at Claremont for forty-eight years (1908–56). His son, Aldo, was one of the amateur golfers who played in the 1937 Oakland Open at Claremont.

Art Graziano succeeded Galletti as superintendent and served until 1972. Stan Burgess was superintendent from 1973 to 1979, when Randy Gai was appointed. Gai is an excellent golfer in addition to being an excellent golf course superintendent. In 1991 the Golf Course Superintendent Association recognized him with a Merit Award for Excellence in Turf Grass Maintenance.

Above: *Jay McDaniel, golf professional*

Right: *Randy Gai, golf course superintendent*

Opposite page, left:  *Northern California Golf Association Open Trophy won by Tal Smith*

Opposite page, top right: *Art Graziano*

Opposite page, bottom right: *Mowing the grass during the early years.*

## TOURNAMENTS OF NOTE
### THE 1937 OAKLAND OPEN

The Oakland Open was held from 1937 through 1944 and was sponsored by the Oakland Junior Chamber of Commerce. Its general chairman was Claremont's own Stuart Hawley Jr., an amateur golfer, and Claremont hosted the tournament in January 1937.

Compared with today's professional tour, the Oakland Open may not seem like much, because the winner's prize was only twelve hundred dollars. However, this was during the Depression, when the number of rounds that were played had declined to about half of that played during the 1920s. The event, a seventy-two-hole tournament that was played in three days, and its public-

ity gave the game a much-needed boost. After 1937 the tournament was held at Sequoyah Country Club, because a lack of fairway fences at Claremont made it impossible to secure the course from fans that did not pay. During those difficult economic times, gate crashing was all too common. Twelve thousand spectators attended the 1937 Oakland Open, but only three thousand paid the three-dollar admission fee. In spite of that, the event covered its expenses and was deemed a success.

The 1937 Oakland Open is best remembered for the man who won it—Samuel Jackson Snead. He was a twenty-four-year-old unknown from the South who had won only four hundred dollars as a professional, and he was

up against the likes of Byron Nelson, Lloyd Mangrum, Craig Wood, Lawson Little, Jimmy Thompson, Ralph Guldahl, Henry Picard, and Johnny Revolta, who were some of the best golfers of that time. It was the first major tournament that Snead had won, and the rest, as they say, is history.

Snead has fond memories of Claremont, and Claremont is proud to be the site of his first tour victory. Sometime after his win, Snead said,

*I remember a little jewel of a course out West in Oakland named Claremont. In 1937, I entered the Oakland Open at Claremont as a wiry unknown pro from West Virginia. I was so unknown they misspelled my name on the pairings list. Well, they sure knew how to spell my name four days later, when they put my name on the winner's check for $1,200. I asked for cash but settled for a check. Anyway . . . I'd sure like to return to Claremont, the site of my first pro win, someday . . .*

**Above:** *Sam Snead at Claremont, 1993*

**Right:** *When Sam Snead won the 1937 Oakland Open at Claremont, he was still an unknown.*

**Opposite page:** *Stuart Hawley Jr.*

And return he did. Snead visited again in 1993 and spent two nights at the Club. He delighted golfers and staff alike at a large reception on the terrace, and he toured the course with John Fite, Hal Lauth, and Club President Tom Hecht. Snead said, *I always considered the 11th hole one of the most beautiful in golf*, and he clearly remembered the 13th hole by saying, *I thought it was one of the hardest par-3s I had ever played.*

### THE SHIPYARD OPEN

During World War II, thousands of people were working at the nine shipyards in the Bay Area. Stuart Hawley Jr., a Claremont member, and Arthur Crist, who later would become a member and who recently related this story to the author, were associated with the shipyards. They also were volunteers who headed sports committees for Bay Area Junior Chambers of Commerce—Crist worked for the San Francisco chamber, and Hawley worked for the Oakland chamber. In 1943 they learned that Dolores Hope, wife of entertainer Bob Hope, was endorsing a war bond sales drive. To aid this effort, Hawley and

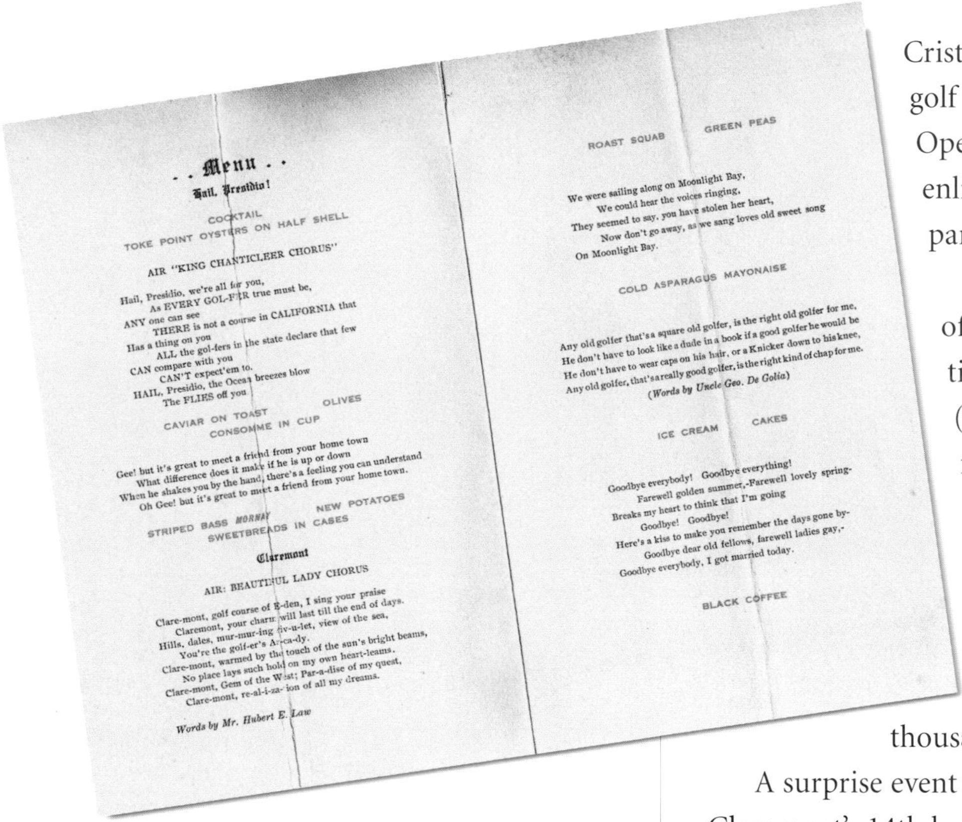

# . . Menu . .

**Hail, Presidio!**

COCKTAIL
TOKE POINT OYSTERS ON HALF SHELL

AIR "KING CHANTICLEER CHORUS"

Hail, Presidio, we're all for you,
As EVERY GOL-FER true must be,
ANY one can see
THERE is not a course in CALIFORNIA that
Has a thing on you
ALL the gol-fers in the state declare that few
CAN compare with you
CAN'T expect'em to.
HAIL, Presidio, the Ocean breezes blow
The FLIES off you

CAVIAR ON TOAST OLIVES
CONSOMME IN CUP

Gee! but it's great to meet a friend from your home town
What difference does it make if he is up or down
When he shakes you by the hand, there's a feeling you can understand
Oh Gee! but it's great to meet a friend from your home town.

STRIPED BASS *MORNAY* NEW POTATOES
SWEETBREADS IN CASES

**Claremont**

AIR: BEAUTIFUL LADY CHORUS

Clare-mont, golf course of E-den, I sing your praise
Claremont, your charm will last till the end of days.
Hills, dales, mur-mur-ing riv-u-let, view of the sea,
You're the golf-er's Ar-ca-dy.
Clare-mont, warmed by the touch of the sun's bright beams,
No place lays such hold on my own heart-leams.
Clare-mont, Gem of the West; Par-a-dise of my quest,
Clare-mont, re-al-i-za-tion of all my dreams.

*Words by Mr. Hubert E. Law*

ROAST SQUAB GREEN PEAS

We were sailing along on Moonlight Bay,
We could hear the voices ringing,
They seemed to say, you have stolen her heart,
Now don't go away, as we sang loves old sweet song
On Moonlight Bay.

COLD ASPARAGUS MAYONAISE

Any old golfer that's a square old golfer, is the right old golfer for me,
He don't have to look like a dude in a book if a good golfer he would be
He don't have to wear caps on his hair, or a Knicker down to his knee,
Any old golfer, that's a really good golfer, is the right kind of chap for me.
(*Words by Uncle Geo. De Golia*)

ICE CREAM CAKES

Goodbye everybody! Goodbye everything!
Farewell golden summer,-Farewell lovely spring-
Breaks my heart to think that I'm going
Goodbye! Goodbye!
Here's a kiss to make you remember the days gone by-
Goodbye dear old fellows, farewell ladies gay,-
Goodbye everybody, I got married today.

BLACK COFFEE

**Above:** ***Menu from "Hail, Presidio!" tournament and dinner***

**Right:** ***California State Open Trophy won by Tal Smith in 1946 (© Joann Dost)***

**Opposite page:** ***Macdonald Smith hits a shot out of the rough during one of his many tournament appearances.***

Crist organized a Junior Chambers of Commerce golf tournament that they named the Shipyard Open. With Mrs. Hope's help, Hawley and Crist enlisted Bob Hope and his pal, Bing Crosby, to participate and to be the featured attraction.

The field consisted of thirty-six entrants, all of whom were shipyard workers. The elimination round was played at Berkeley Golf Club (present-day Mira Vista), and the prize for the four finalists' was the chance to play with Hope and Crosby. Two finalists played nine holes at Claremont, and the other two played nine holes with Hope and Crosby at Presidio Golf Club. The public paid a one-dollar entrance fee, and nearly eight thousand dollars was raised.

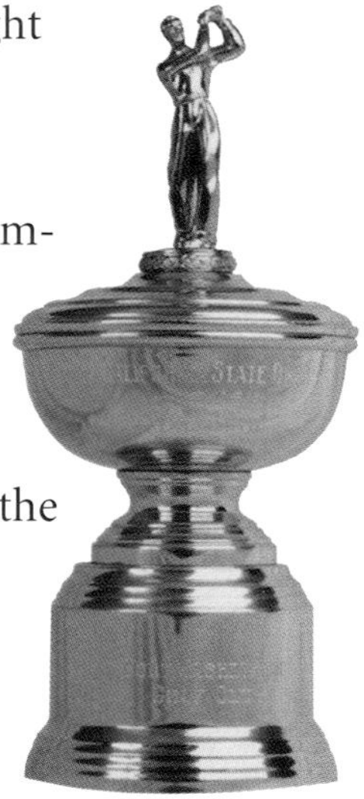

A surprise event was staged near the green on Claremont's 14th hole, where a piano and an accompanist were waiting. After Crosby, Hope, and the two finalists hit their second shots, Crosby moved toward the piano and announced that he would sing and Hope would dance if someone in the crowd would step forward and purchase a one-hundred-thousand-dollar war bond. No one was prepared to buy a bond of such value, yet one gentleman came forth and announced that he would make the purchase. The crowd gasped, and the pianist began to play. While Crosby sang "Avalon," Hope did his part with a soft-shoe dance. After that, Crosby landed his second shot on the green and sank a birdie putt. It was later determined that the big purchase had been staged—the buyer was a Bank of America employee who had arranged to make the purchase in an effort to encourage the sale of war bonds.

## NOTABLE CLAREMONT GOLFERS

James "Pop" Smith, Claremont's first greenskeeper, had five famous golfing sons: George, Macdonald, Willie, Alex, and James Jr. George Smith had been steward of the Oakland Golf Club prior to becoming Claremont's first golf professional. Macdonald Smith, who also taught at Claremont, is held in great esteem in his birthplace of Carnoustie, Scotland, because he won numerous major tournaments in Great Britain and the United States. He was born in Carnoustie in 1890 and learned the game on those challenging links. After a string of notable performances in local competitions there, he immigrated to America in 1908. He settled in northern California, where he worked for his brother, George, at Claremont Country Club and at the Hotel Del Monte. Macdonald won the Oakland Open in 1910, and he and his brothers, Alex and Willie, either won or were runners-up in

Above: *Macdonald Smith*

Right: *Jack Neville, five-time winner of the California State Amateur Championship*

Opposite page: *Early Men's Club Championship, 1935 (© Joann Dost)*

the U.S. Open nine times. Willie won the U.S. Open in 1899, and Alex won it three times in 1906, 1907, and 1910.

Among Macdonald's students was Jack Neville, a five-time winner of the California State Amateur Championship who later designed the Pebble Beach Golf Links. Neville's training for both golf and course design was the result of his father, John, serving as a Claremont Country Club greenskeeper.

Jim Barnes, who was nicknamed "Long Jim" for his hitting distance, also taught at Claremont. He was champion of the first two PGA tournaments in 1916 and 1919 (there were no PGA tournaments in 1917 and 1918), the U.S. Open in 1921, and the British Open in 1925.

Golfers connected with Oakland Golf Club and then Claremont Country Club were among the few that dominated the game during the early years of golf in the United States. They won or were runners-up twenty times in the first thirty-four U.S. Open tournaments, which began in 1895. In a recently produced video about its first hundred years, the NCGA commented on the many famous golfers at Claremont and stated Claremont was *the course where the champions lived.*

In later years Claremont continued to produce many outstanding golfers. Don Haslett became a Claremont golf legend in his own time by winning the Club Championship eleven times over a span of thirty-two years from 1947 through 1979. He also won the President's Cup five times over twenty-nine years from 1948 through 1977. Before Claremont, Haslett and Tal Smith, who were the same age, competed against each other on their respective Piedmont and Alameda High School golf teams, and Haslett won the NCGA Junior Championship in 1936.

Next in line for total Club Championship wins is a tie between Frank Kales and Richard Stevenson. Both won it six times—Kales during the 1920s, and Stevenson between 1939 and 1967.

Stuart Hawley Jr. was another top golfer. He played at Stanford and won the NCGA Junior Championship in 1932, and in 1934 he won the NCGA Amateur Championship and the California State Amateur Championship. Not satisfied with being on the sidelines during World War II, Hawley joined the Navy in 1944. Tragically, he was killed in action as the result of a Kamikaze attack on his ship. Claremont had twenty-seven

Above: *Arthur Selby and his son, John "Jack" Selby*

Right: *Stuart Hawley Jr. Memorial Trophy (© Joann Dost)*

members who served in the military, and Hawley was the only one to die in action. To honor his memory, the Board of Directors approved the purchase of a trophy that was given to the NCGA for use as an award for future champions. This trophy is displayed at the NCGA Headquarters in Poppy Hills.

Another successful amateur golfer is Jack Selby, who is the only Claremont member to have played in the Masters Tournament. Selby qualified for the 1948 tournament after he became a semi-finalist in the 1947 U.S. Amateur Championship at Pebble Beach.

Former Club President Richard Railsback (1973–74) also played with distinction. In 1929 he won the California State Junior Championship. As a member of Sequoyah Country Club, he won the Club Championship twice in 1938 and 1939; as a member of Claremont, he won the Club Championship in 1966.

George H. Kelly won the Club Championship eight years in a row from 1988 to 1995. He also won the Oak Tree Classic six times, including a streak of five consecutive wins from 1988 through 1992.

Bobbie Dawson Hartson achieved distinction playing women's golf. She was a great amateur and was one of the best long-ball hitters of her time. Hartson won the California State Women's Open three times in 1953, 1956, and 1957, and she was president of the Women's Trans-National Golf Association in 1964 and 1965. During World War II, Hartson served as a Women's Army Corps pilot.

Sally Tomlinson, who learned golf under the instruction of Dewey Longworth, won the Ladies' Club Championship for the eighteenth time in 2002. She has played in the Women's Trans-National Championship for thirty-one consecutive years and is currently that organization's president. In 1995 Tomlinson won the California State Seniors Open at Laguna Seca. Both Hartson and Tomlinson have twice won the Women's Golf Association of Northern California Championship.

Other winners at Claremont include Mrs. Miles Griffin, who won the Club Championship eight times, and Elizbeth Elliot, who won it seven times. Two other members—Mrs. Wyman Taylor and Molly Crowley—each have won the Club Championship six times.

A summary of golf at Claremont would not be complete without mentioning Weller Noble, Claremont's own "Doctor of Golf." Noble was an outstanding golfer and coach. He exemplified the true sportsmanship of the game when he said, *You can never be a total master of golf. You must remember that golf will always be your master.* Ironically, Noble almost achieved the impossible. Between

**Above:** *Richard Railsback*

**Left:** *Sally Tomlinson*

*Weller Noble with his trophies (© Joann Dost)*

Right: *Young golfers, 1938. The child on the far right is four-year-old Jackie Palmer. (© Joann Dost)*

the ages of sixty-four and seventy-eight, he shot his age or better at least once each year. When he was seventy-six, he scored seventy-six or better on eighty-four of the one hundred sixty-seven rounds of golf he played. He played 2,426 rounds between 1955 and 1969, when his average score per round was 75.2. During the President's Cup dinner on April 24, 1970, Claremont conferred upon Noble the honorary "Doctor of Golf" degree. Following Noble's death in 1977, the U.S. Seniors Golf Association (USSGA) established the Weller Noble Trophy, which is presented each year to the winner of the International Team matches that are sponsored by the USSGA. The trophy is an impressive and fitting tribute to a man whose memory has become a vital part of Claremont Country Club's history.

*Junior golfers, circa 1930s (© Joann Dost)*

Above, from left to right; *William E. Wood,*
*R. M. Fitzgerald, E. A. Hassan, W. Preston,*
*Robert R. Yates, Frank Kales, Harry Struthers,*
*and Oscar Morgan, circa 1920s. (© Joann Dost)*

Right: *Jack Selby's tee prize from*
*1948 Masters Tournament (© Joann Dost)*

Far right: *Edward Rix, circa 1910.*
*Rix was the Club's president in 1913.*

**Far left, top:** *E. A. Rix Perpetual Trophy*

**Far left, bottom:** *Ladies' President's Cup (© Joann Dost)*

**Left:** *The 1935 report to the membership listed the number of rounds of golf that had been played annually since 1921.*

## TO THE MEMBERS OF THE CLAREMONT COUNTRY CLUB:

Our operations during 1935 indicate that except as relating to loss in revenue from dues and green fees, the general operation of the Club compares favorably with the 1934 operation.

### FINANCES

A payment of $10,000 was made, account of the mortgage, and the necessary payments, account of the Quarry and Clifton Street purchases, leaving a net amount now due for that account of $7,321.82.

During the year 1935 the gross operating income was $167,131.03 as against $172,190.38 for 1934, a loss of $5,059.35. This was the result of decreased patronage and decreased income from dues and green fees.

The expense of operating the various departments was $155,549.02 as against $154,628.46, an increase of $920.56 over the previous year.

After deducting other income and expense not relating to operations, the net for the year was $6,108.07, a decrease as compared with 1934 of $2,192.60.

### MEMBERSHIP

During 1935 24 regular members were elected.

### GOLF

The records for 1935 indicate 25,846 games were played, with a total of $17,069.20 paid to caddies. The green fees amounted to $4,892.00 as against $5,633.50 for 1934, a loss of $741.50 for the year.

Our experience at Claremont, and reports received from other clubs throughout the country, indicate a material decline in golf activities by members of golf clubs.

I have located old schedules indicating operations at Claremont. Although some years are missing, the data available will probably be of interest to our members:

| Year | No. of Members Playing | Green Fee Receipts |
|------|-----------------------|--------------------|
| 1921 | 60,081 | $ 5,798.00 |
| 1922 | 60,599 | 6,294.50 |
| 1926 | 45,646 | 9,046.00 |
| 1927 | 43,997 | 6,680.00 |
| 1929 | 59,755 | 10,288.00 |
| 1930 | 50,245 | 9,452.00 |
| 1931 | 39,700 | 8,240.25 |
| 1932 | 36,315 | 7,209.00 |
| 1933 | 32,292 | 5,177.00 |
| 1934 | 26,565 | 5,633.50 |
| 1935 | 25,246 | 4,872.00 |

### TENNIS

Two new tennis courts have been completed with other area available, should activities warrant such construction and the Directors decide to add additional units.

### GENERAL OPERATION

It was not necessary to purchase water for irrigating purposes during 1935. This saving is accounted for under our golf course expenses, and it would appear reasonably certain that sufficient water is now impounded in our reservoir to insure an ample supply, probably for all future time.

### MT. DIABLO COUNTRY CLUB PROPOSAL

As this is written, the Directors have not reached a conclusion as to the purchase of the Mt Diablo Country Club properties, which have been offered to Claremont free of encumbrance for approximately $30,000.

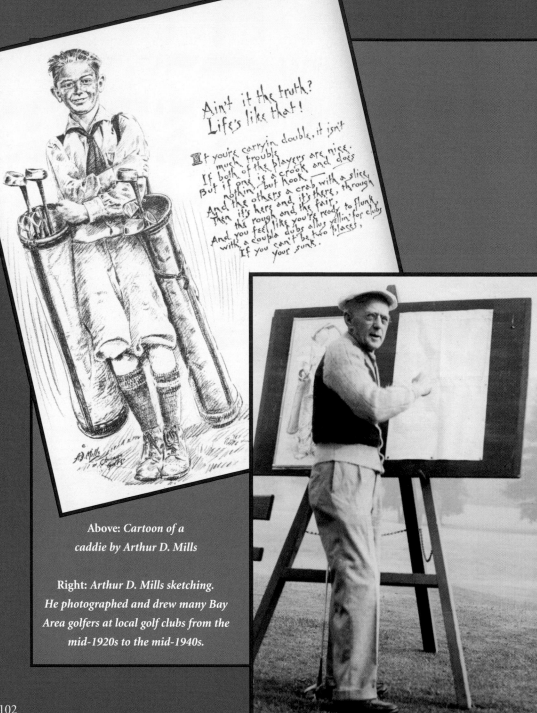

Ain't it the truth?
Life's like that!

If you're carryin double, it isn't
        much trouble
If both of the players are nice.
But if one is a crook and does
        nothin' but hook —
And the others a crab with a slice,
Then it's here and it's there, through
        the rough and the fair,
And you feel like you're ready to flunk.
With a coupla dubs allus yellin' for clubs,
If you can't be two places,
        your sunk.

**Above:** *Cartoon of a caddie by Arthur D. Mills*

**Right:** *Arthur D. Mills sketching. He photographed and drew many Bay Area golfers at local golf clubs from the mid-1920s to the mid-1940s.*

**Above:** *Bert Railey (© Joann Dost)*

**Above:** *Robert M. Fitzgerald and Ed Parrish (© Joann Dost)*

**Center:** *Robert M. Fitzgerald at 14th stone tee (© Joann Dost)*

**Right:** *Vernon Hardy (© Joann Dost)*

103

Above: *Junior golf program*

Right: *Men's Invitational Golf Tournament Trophy (© Joann Dost)*

Opposite page: *Rich Straass, assistant golf professional*

## CLAREMONT'S GOLF PROGRAM TODAY

About thirty thousand rounds of golf are played annually at the Club. This is about half the number of rounds that were played during the 1920s, when members would play eighteen holes in the morning, have lunch, and then play another eighteen holes in the afternoon. This was easily accomplished, because play was faster then. Golfers walked with their caddies and were prepared to hit when they reached their balls. Playing eighteen holes in three hours was common. Today, Claremont is one of the few clubs in the area where caddies are still available.

Claremont has four major men's golf tournaments: the Club Championship, the President's Cup, the Oak Tree Classic, and the two-day Invitational. The Club Championship is match play, and this seeded tournament is played in September. Members with the lowest handicaps are in the Championship Flight; the other flights are determined by handicaps. The winner of the Championship Flight is the official Club Champion.

The President's Cup is a match-play tournament that is played in the spring. Players are assigned to flights that are determined by handicaps. The Oak Tree Classic, which is now held in May, is stroke play. The two-day Invitational is a member-guest event (net score, par point). The team's best ball is played on the first day, and both balls are played on the second.

The women's golf program also has four major golf tournaments. The women's Club Championship uses the same format as the men's; the women's President's Cup is match play and is held in the spring concurrently with the men's President's Cup; and the women's two-day Invitational is held mid-week in June. The women also have their own Tal Smith Cup tournament.

Both the men and women golfers at Claremont continue an active home-and-home schedule with other local private clubs. These tournaments date back to the

Above: *Golf items from
Claremont's past (© Joann Dost)*

Opposite page: *Claremont's golf course, 2002
(© Eureka Cartography)*

early rivalries between Oakland Golf Club and San Francisco Golf Club and later rivalries with Sequoyah, Orinda, and Diablo Country Clubs. Claremont also has a junior golf program that dates back to the late 1920s. Junior golf clinics are held each summer for two weeks, and the annual Junior Championship is played in May.

Many other tournaments take place at Claremont throughout the year. Sixty-four two-man teams compete from March until October for the men's Four-Ball Championship. There also are Twilight Tournaments, Scrambles, and one-day Invitationals in addition to the Big Game, the East-West Locker Rooms, and the Father-Son/Daughter Tournaments.

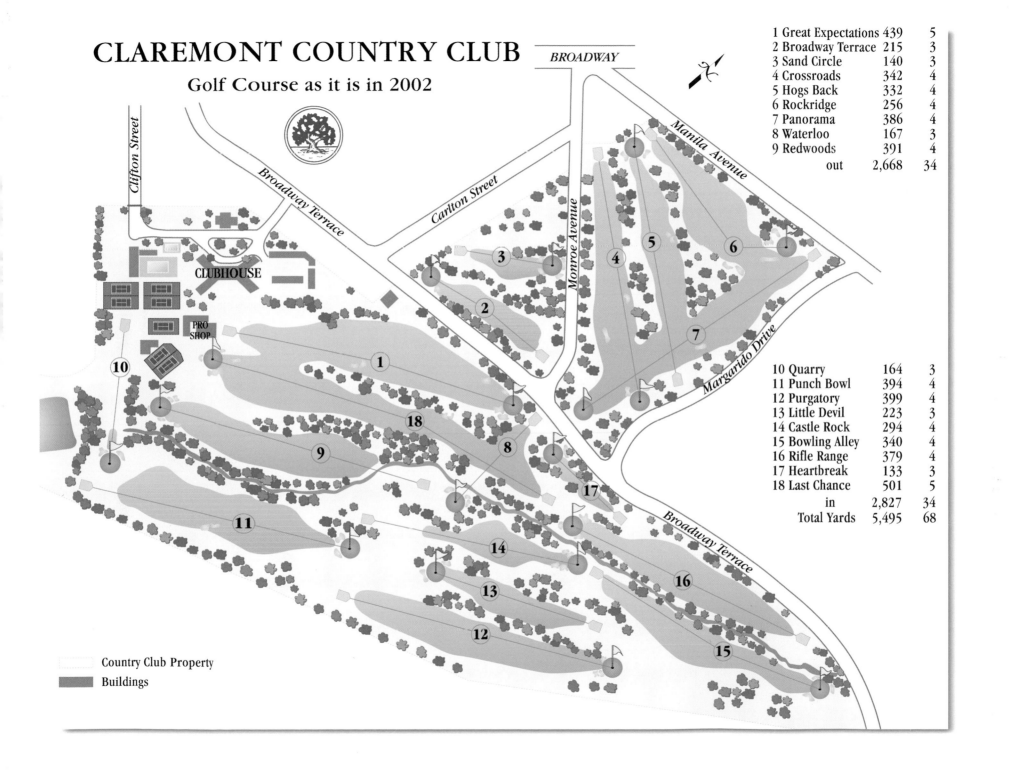

# CLAREMONT COUNTRY CLUB

## Golf Course as it is in 2002

BROADWAY

Clifton Street

Broadway Terrace

Carlton Street

Monroe Avenue

Manila Avenue

Margarido Drive

Broadway Terrace

CLUBHOUSE

PRO SHOP

| | | | |
|---|---|---|---|
| 1 | Great Expectations | 439 | 5 |
| 2 | Broadway Terrace | 215 | 3 |
| 3 | Sand Circle | 140 | 3 |
| 4 | Crossroads | 342 | 4 |
| 5 | Hogs Back | 332 | 4 |
| 6 | Rockridge | 256 | 4 |
| 7 | Panorama | 386 | 4 |
| 8 | Waterloo | 167 | 3 |
| 9 | Redwoods | 391 | 4 |
| | out | 2,668 | 34 |

| | | | |
|---|---|---|---|
| 10 | Quarry | 164 | 3 |
| 11 | Punch Bowl | 394 | 4 |
| 12 | Purgatory | 399 | 4 |
| 13 | Little Devil | 223 | 3 |
| 14 | Castle Rock | 294 | 4 |
| 15 | Bowling Alley | 340 | 4 |
| 16 | Rifle Range | 379 | 4 |
| 17 | Heartbreak | 133 | 3 |
| 18 | Last Chance | 501 | 5 |
| | in | 2,827 | 34 |
| | Total Yards | 5,495 | 68 |

Country Club Property

Buildings

Above: *Caddie Gary Morgan*

Opposite page, left to right: *Lee Smith,
Charles Gaines, Charles Williams, Ron Riddle,
Louis Ramos, Tim Zukas, and Ron Mason.*

## CADDIES

One thing that sets Claremont apart from most other golf clubs is its caddie program. Claremont has had caddies since it was the Oakland Golf Club, and while motorized carts have taken over most courses today, Claremont has tried to balance the need for carts with its desire to maintain the traditions of the game.

Good caddies add to the tradition, color, and enjoyment of golf. Far more than just golf club carriers, caddies can be very helpful to the average player by suggesting the right club, by computing distances, and by suggesting strategies for play. This also allows the player to walk, and, in addition to good exercise, it provides the golfer with a straight-line perspective for pondering the next shot.

There is some generally unknown humor amongst the caddies at Claremont, and on occasion they play tricks on each other. For instance, there is the rock-in-the-bag gag, where rocks are concealed in clothing and are added to another caddie's bag. Unless the rocks are discovered in advance, the unsuspecting caddie carries the added weight for eighteen holes. Another gag involves the flagstick. On damp days caddies have been known to stick the damp end of the flagstick in sand and then place the gritty end into the cup liner. Naturally, when the next caddie comes along and removes the flagstick, it takes such force that the whole cup liner often comes up with it.

Claremont has had some caddies with exceptionally long terms of service. Ron Riddle has been at Claremont off and on for forty-eight years, Tim Zukas has served the Club for thirty-seven years, and Louis Ramos has been with the Club for thirty-three years. Others with seniority include Charles Gaines, twelve years; Lee Smith, nine years; Ron Mason, eight years; and Charles Williams, six years. The Club encourages hiring caddies whenever possible. Not only will this practice help to maintain this unique corps of people, it also will continue the tradition of the game.

Tennis has been a part of Claremont Country Club from the beginning. The Club's opening festivities on December 4, 1904, included *a tennis tourney between some of the best players in the State.* The surface of the first two tennis courts was made of compacted seashells, which was considered to be the finest type of surface at that time. A scow load of shells was purchased and was shipped from Monterey Bay just for this purpose. These courts remain in their original location behind the 18th green, although the shell surface has long since been replaced.

A third tennis court was added in 1926 and was located where the main court for instruction is today, which is opposite the tennis shop. Even though the game of tennis was properly called lawn tennis, that new court had a clay surface. Courts four and five were added as part of the 1950 improvement program, and courts six and seven were built in 1977. They replaced what was then a practice putting green and what had originally been

installed as a green for lawn bowling. Extensive renovations to the courts in 1997 and 1999 included the installation of lighting for night play.

The Pat O'Hara Tennis Shop was built in 1970 and was dedicated to the memory of the Club's second tennis pro. It has a lounge and a snack bar for the tennis players, and these facilities are used by many of the golfers when they make the turn at the 10th tee. The tennis shop and the addition of courts six and seven reflected the rapid growth of Claremont members' interest in tennis during the 1960s and 1970s. Although tennis at Claremont enjoys a rich heritage, the records of tennis activities before the 1927 clubhouse fire are sketchy.

## TENNIS PROFESSIONALS

Tom Stow was hired as Claremont's first tennis professional in 1932. When he was a student at the University of California, Berkeley, Stow won the National College Athletic Association (NCAA) Doubles Championship in 1926 with Claremont's Edward G. "Bud" Chandler as his partner. Stow was an excellent teacher, and his more notable pupils included Don Budge, Margaret Osborne, and Dorothy Head Knode. Most famous was Budge, who won the tennis grand slam—Wimbledon, the U.S. Open, the Australian Open, and the French Open—in 1938. Budge was not a member of Claremont, but during the 1930s he was a regular at Claremont while taking lessons from Stow.

Stow's presence at Claremont kept the interest in tennis very much alive during the otherwise dreary years of the Great Depression. He arranged many tennis exhibitions and tournaments that were high-class affairs and were well attended and appreciated by the members. In addition to the serious competitions, there were theme tournaments as well.

Stow left Claremont in 1942 to become the head professional and later the general manager of Berkeley Tennis Club. His successor was Pat O'Hara, who served as the tennis professional at Claremont for twenty-three years. He was a native Australian who came to the United States as a professional golfer. O'Hara was the tennis professional at Coronado Beach and Tennis Club before coming to Claremont, and his focus was on teaching the basics. He had a strong loyalty to Claremont and was very good with young people. His instruction included good court manners, which he felt should always be part of a sound tennis game. O'Hara's wife, Florence, helped run the original tennis shop, which was located in the present-day junior tennis players' clubroom. O'Hara retired in 1964.

Facing page: *Tom Stow, Claremont's first tennis professional*

Left: *Tom Stow and Don Budge*

Below: *Claremont's members enjoy first-rate tennis facilities.*

Above: *Pat O'Hara was Claremont's tennis professional for twenty-three years.*

Right: *John Hilton and Bob Hammerlee*

For less than a year, E. Martin "Blackie" Jones, who earlier had taught tennis at West Point, served as the tennis professional. Several assistants helped during this period, including Jack Elliott, a versatile Claremont member who later became president of the Northern California Golf Association. After Jones left Claremont, the job went to Dennis Burchell, who served from 1966 to 1968. Burchell was followed by Mike Sheridan until 1970, when John Hilton became Claremont's head tennis professional. Hilton, who came to Claremont from Menlo Circus Club, learned to play as well as to teach under the tutelage of John Gardiner in Carmel Valley. Hilton was Claremont's head tennis professional for the next twenty-five years until he retired in 1995. Paul Garron, who had replaced Bob Hammerlee as the assistant tennis professional, became the head professional after Hilton retired and served through 1998.

After an extensive search, Steve Shaw was appointed head tennis professional in 1999. His experience included collegiate play, two years on the Open and Satellite Class Tours, and twelve years as a teaching professional. Paul Isurin is the assistant tennis professional today, and he and Shaw lead a dynamic tennis program with enthusiasm and innovative ideas.

## NOTABLE TENNIS MEMBERS

There are many Claremont members who have distinguished themselves in the world of tennis. The mention of a few names will almost surely result in the unwarranted omission of others, but some members cannot be overlooked. Bud Chandler was already an authentic living legend when he joined Claremont in 1965. He had won the NCAA Singles Championships in 1925 and 1926, and he also had teamed with Tom Stow to win the NCAA Doubles Championship in 1926. That year Chandler was ranked fifth in the United States; in 1930, 1931, and 1932 he was ranked first in northern California. Chandler and Gerry Stratford became

Above: *Rupe Ricksen, Hugh Ditzler,*
*Bud Chandler, and Gerry Stratford*

Right: *Ball boys taking a break, circa 1950s*

Opposite page: *Social tennis groups*

one of the best and most enduring doubles teams in history: they won the National Doubles Championship in the thirty-five-year, forty-five-year (three years in a row), sixty-year, sixty-five-year, and seventy-five-year age brackets. Chandler is in the Northern California Tennis Hall of Fame and the University of California, Berkeley, Athletic Hall of Fame.

Harper Massie was a Pacific Coast junior doubles champion in 1935 and 1936. Paul Newton was an NCAA doubles champion, and he was one of Tom Stow's players at the University of California, Berkeley, who often rallied with Don Budge at Claremont. Newton and his partner, Richard Bennett, won the NCAA Doubles Championship in 1935 and 1937 and were inducted into the Northern California Tennis Hall of Fame in 1978.

Hugh Ditzler's National and Northern California Doubles Championships with Cliff Mayne spanned four decades from the National Intercollegiate Championship in 1952 through the National Men's 35 and 45 Championships during the 1960s, 1970s, and 1980s. In 1999 Ditzler

was inducted into the Northern California Tennis Hall of Fame. Rupe Ricksen, who was Claremont's 1985–86 president, has been ranked high nationally many times during the thirty-five years he partnered with Ditzler and twin brother John Ricksen. Rupe and John were a top-national intercollegiate team at the University of California, Berkeley, and Rupe and Hugh were ranked number one in the Northern California Men's 45. The Ricksen brothers and Ditzler have all been inducted into the University of California, Berkeley, Athletic Hall of Fame.

Mark McKeen competed as a junior and won the California 18 and Under Singles Championship in 1980. He was ranked number one in both singles and doubles for northern California, and at Stanford he was a four-year starter on the team that won the NCAA Championship in both 1981 and 1983.

In 1987 Dr. John Adams, knee brace and all, was ranked twenty-third in the Northern California Men's 70 Singles. In 1997 Kristi Roemer was ranked number one in the Northern California Girls' 14.

*Junior tennis players, 2001*

*Beginners' tennis instruction*

119

## TENNIS TODAY

Claremont's current tennis program offers a wide variety of men's, women's, and mixed events. Some tournaments, including the annual Team Calcutta and the Wimbledon Wood Classic, are held for both fun and socialization. The Club Championships are more competitive.

Claremont also fields a number of teams that compete in U.S. Tennis Association and Bay Area leagues. The program for juniors includes lessons, year-round competition with other east-bay teams, and fun tournaments. Each summer more than three hundred fifty juniors enroll in Camp Claremont, which includes tennis and golf instruction in the morning and swimming and CPR training in the afternoon.

*Bay Area Ladies' League Champions, 1994*

**Right** (left to right): *Scott Hill and Jim Stehr were the winners of the1996 Men's Doubles Championship, and Spencer Brush and Bob Albo Jr. were the runners-up.*

**Bottom right** (left to right): *Keith MacKenzie, Lorraine Gordon, Carey James (captain), and Chris Bene were the winners of the 2001 Calcutta Tournament.*

**Below** (left to right): *Geoff Hayes, Bill Frizell, Wayne Harbert, and John Whalen were the winners of Men's Biathlon in 2002.*

## SWIMMING AT CLAREMONT

A significant turning point in Claremont's history came with the 1949 decision to build a swimming pool. The idea had been discussed as early as the mid-1930s, and pressure from the membership intensified after World War II. The proposal to borrow fifty thousand dollars for the construction of a pool was approved after considerable debate, and a 36' x 75' swimming pool was opened during the summer of 1950. The pool was later equipped with a diving board, and small inner tubes were provided for the younger swimmers' enjoyment. It has become a tradition for these swimmers to participate in the annual Fourth of July inner tube races and diving contests.

Henry "Hank" Squires, an Oakland grammar school principal, was hired to manage the pool. During Squire's twenty-five years of service at Claremont, he taught hundreds of children how to swim and how to safely participate in pool activities. As the membership increased, the pool became the place for families to gather.

In 1975 Al Thurling, a teacher and a coach at Acalanes High School in Lafayette (California), replaced Squires. Thurling took over the management of the pool with his daughter, Karen. In the years that followed, both water volleyball and water basketball were added to the pool's program for the growing number of children, and a lane was designated for swimming laps. In 1985 Karen became manager of both the swimming pool and the snack bar

Facing page: *Claremont's swimming pool and clubhouse*

123

facility. In recent years she and the Swim Committee have worked hard to improve the quality and the general atmosphere of the pool area, including the variety of food. (Karen's brother, Ross, is a twelve-year employee who works in the golf pro shop).

In 1987 a small shallow pool was added to provide a safe water experience for the ever-increasing number of toddlers and less-experienced young swimmers. This area is set apart from the main pool, which provides a quieter area for parents to both watch and enjoy their young children as they begin to explore a new water environment. The deepest point is only three feet, and there are stairs and hand railings to guide small children.

Holiday celebrations and informal theme dinners have been added for families to enjoy during the summer and early fall. Improved food service and sound systems have made these events very popular. Also during the summer, the pool staff enthusiastically participates in the afternoon activities of Camp Claremont.

Facing page, left: *Henry "Hank" Squires managed Claremont's pool for twenty-five years.*

Facing page, right: *Al Thurling and his daughter, Karen (left), succeeded Hank Squires.*

*Claremont's toddler pool*

*The main pool, built in 1950, is
enjoying a resurgence in popularity.*

# CLAREMONT TODAY

## CHAPTER 9

Claremont still stands in the same "sunshine of success" that warmed Edwin Goodall when he wrote the first "President's Report" for the members in 1906. The Club has not just weathered economic downturns, wars, and fires, it has prospered in spite of these events. Claremont's presence and beauty are great assets to the city of Oakland and the entire Bay Area community. The belief of Claremont's founders that the Club must be *a large and popular club* remains the key to its continued success. The Club is family oriented and has facilities and social events for all ages. Today, Claremont Country Club employs some one hundred ten people in both full- and part-time capacities, and the employees all are appreciated by the members for the high level of service that they provide throughout the year.

Claremont's clubhouse and grounds are elegant and well maintained. In addition to golf, swimming, and tennis facilities, the Club has guest rooms, lounges, dining rooms, and reception

areas that can accommodate a wide variety of functions. In 2001 the Club's communications capability was expanded with the creation of a members-only confidential Web site. All sorts of information about Club activities is available electronically via the Internet.

In 2003 there were five hundred regular members plus various other categories for tennis, social, and junior membership. Combined, there were eight hundred total members who, along with their spouses and children, created a base of over two thousand potential participants for Club activities. A recent survey has shown there are many current members whose families have been members of Claremont for several generations.

*Above and opposite page: Claremont's clubhouse has unique architecture and a picturesque setting. (© Joann Dost)*

*Right: Alec Churchward, general manager*

Fortunately, Claremont has been blessed with officers, directors, and committee members who were dedicated to their Club and their assignments. With this good governance and a full membership, Claremont Country Club will continue to achieve the motto of its predecessor, the Oakland Golf Club, and *"Keep the Ball a Rolling."*

Above: *Golf shop and tennis courts*

Right: *The dining room is an elegant setting for parties.* (© James Brian Fidelibus)

Opposite page, left: *Commemorative plaques can be found on a large rock near the pro shop.*

Opposite page, right: *The next generation*

Facing page: *Children's holiday party, 2001*

Left: *At certain times of year, the cherry blossoms highlight the property.*

Below: *Deer often graze on Claremont's grounds.*

Above: *18th fairway (© Joann Dost)*

Facing page: *View from the clubhouse*

138

Above: *13th green*

Right: *13th old stone
tee with 14th green below*

Facing page: *11th hole—
green to tee (© Joann Dost)*

Above and opposite page: *14th fairway and green* (© Joann Dost)

Facing page: *9th fairway separated by creek (© Joann Dost)*

Left: *15th green*

Below: *16th hole*

6th fairway to green (© Joann Dost)

*3rd hole*

*Claremont Country Club staff, 2002*

## CHAPTER 10

The history of Claremont Country Club is more than just a timeline of events. It also is about people. The earlier chapters discussed the members, their activities, and their accomplishments. Equally important to Claremont's one-hundred-year success is the loyal, hardworking staff—both past and present.

Many of these fine people work behind the scenes and serve in positions that do not require direct contact with the members. Yet, each and every employee performs his or her job for the direct benefit of the Club and the enjoyment of the members. From the gardeners who maintain the grounds and grow the flowers for the dining room tables to the housekeepers who maintain the beautiful bedrooms upstairs, each employee is dedicated to serving the Club and its members.

Claremont has one hundred ten full-time and part-time employees. Nearly 60 percent of these people have ten or more years of service with the Club, and eight employees have been

*Jim Kane*

*Luisa Irvin*

working at Claremont for twenty years or longer. Don Davis, a golf course spray technician, retired in 2002 after a remarkable forty-nine years of service! These statistics show the Club offers good and diverse employment opportunities, and the members benefit from the long-term dedication of many fine employees.

In addition to service longevity, many employees are related to each other, which adds a unique family association within the Claremont clan. Relationships include husbands and wives, siblings, and cousins. Some have worked their way up to key positions, while others are beginning their careers through on-the-job training.

Claremont Country Club's employees at the close of 2002 are listed below by department. The numbers of years of service are listed beside those employees who have been with the Club *five years or more.*

**Above:** *Javier Rodriguez*

**Right:** *Robert Cortez*

**General Manager**
Alec R. Churchward—15

**Office**
Mary Anne Aiello—21
Kaity Booth
Susan Butler—5
Nettie Koo
Linda Lerch
Linda Saefong
Steve Sharp—7
Som Sin
Chuck Sturtevant—7

**Catering**
Rosie Bonds—12
Aloy Catolos
Sakul Chaloeicheep
Brenda Chester—5
Ramon Chua
Jason Chung
Peter Chung—8
Luis Co
Maria Condor
Annie Cortez—20
Ed Duldulao—8
Keith Fang
Ben Garcia
Bijay Gautam
Yong Guan
Michael Lam

Louise Lampkin—13
May Lee
Danny Leung
Lucita Love—5
Squirt Lunk
Michele Meillon-Svane—18
Manuel Munos
Jonas Pamintuan—6
Jun Rafanan—5
Bonnie Sita
Julie Trincado—8
Martin Tse
Ellen Wen—6
Alice Ye
Johnny Yeung

**Lockers**
Joey Estandian—6
Jesus Solis—16

**Bellmen**
Cisco Badiolo
John Hanaoka—25
Carlo Marcelo—6
Anton Sargento

**Clubhouse**
Juan Carlos Bautista Rojas
Danny Garcia
Jose Jimenez Perez
Tito Perez
Rick Terlesky—17

**Golf Course**
Juan Berrios—7
Carlos DeLeon
Pete Fleming
Randy Gai—28

Vidal Jimenez Perez
Jim Kane—7
Elio Ledesma Sr.
Elio Ledesma Jr.
Danny Pilat—13
Lee Smith
Joe Teixeira—30
Chris Woborny—9

**Golf Shop**
Richard Hudner
Christine Kim
Dennis Lodes
Jay McDaniel
Alfredo Rodriguez—5
Javier Rodriguez
Rich Straass—18
Ross Thurling—12
James Wang

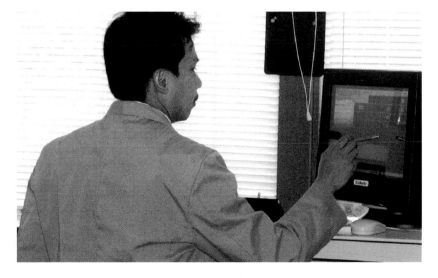

Above: *Rolando Cortez*

Right: *Annie Cortez*

### Tennis

Lindsey Davis
Alex Gallo
Devin Gallo
Paul Isurin
Steve Shaw
Victor Villalpando

### Kitchen

Efrain Arellano
Olegario Cardenas Delapaz
Eloy Garcia
Robert Gee—7
Efrain Gutierrez—12
Gustavo Gutierrez—15
Hugo Gutierrez—11
Tim Jefferson
Graciano Maya
Luis Mendez
Francisco Naranjo
Kin Chung Poon—19
Jose Salazar
Roberto Salazar
Alan Schalmo

### Grounds

Felipe Alcober—11
Rod Gutierrez—22

### Bartenders

Rufino Aquino—10
Robert Cortez—18
Rolando Cortez—25
Omar Fontillas
Gil Gregorio
Nonie Rama—14
Rey Ravanera

### Swimming Pool

Christina Carrington
Tommy Thach
Karen Thurling—16

### Rooms

Sonia Gonzales Carrillo
Luisa Irvin—28
Imelda Quintanilla—12
Barbara Wong—7

Above: *Peter Chung*

Center: *Mary Anne Aiello*

Left: *Michele Svane*

## Presidents of Oakland Golf Club and Claremont Country Club

| | | | | | |
|---|---|---|---|---|---|
| 1897–02 | Orestes Pierce (captain) | 1944–45 | Gerald B. Trayner | 1975–76 | Donald F. Dorward |
| 1903–05 | Edwin Goodall | 1946 | Frank J. Reagan | 1977–78 | Charles F. Jonas |
| 1906 | Frank M. Wilson | 1947 | H. A. Jackson/E. D. Turner Jr. | 1979–80 | C. Lee Emerson Jr. |
| 1907 | Tyler Henshaw | 1948–50 | E. P. Crossan | 1981–82 | Lyle Sampson |
| 1908 | Robert M. Fitzgerald | 1951–53 | Edward W. Engs Jr. | 1983–84 | Jack E. Hooper |
| 1909 | William Pierce Johnson | 1954–56 | Herbert I. Dunn | 1985–86 | Rupert H. Ricksen |
| 1910 | Sam Bell McKee | 1957 | Edward M. Downer Jr. | 1987–88 | Jerry L. Becker |
| 1911–12 | George W. McNear | 1958–59 | Frank H. Barnett | 1989–90 | William J. Logan |
| 1913 | Edward Austin Rix | 1960–61 | William H. Mordy | 1991–92 | Grant B. Powell |
| 1914–15 | William Pierce Johnson | 1962–63 | Herriot Small | 1993–94 | Kenneth G. Hecht Jr. |
| 1916–33 | Robert M. Fitzgerald | 1964–66 | Thomas Ashby | 1995–96 | Grant M. Inman |
| 1934–35 | Vernon S. Hardy | 1967–68 | Eugene D. Sweetland | 1997–98 | Denis P. Mahoney |
| 1936–38 | Bert W. Railey | 1969–70 | J. Marcus Hardin | 1999–00 | Peter D. Scott |
| 1939–40 | Hal W. Force | 1971–72 | Carl E. Simon Jr. | 2001–02 | Philip V. Sarkisian |
| 1941–43 | Charles C. Keeney | 1973–74 | Dr. Richard M. Railsback | 2003 | Warren A. "Chip" Brown |

# Oakland Golf Club/Claremont Country Club—Management

## Club Managers

Mrs. R. Bruegger, 1898–02 (clubhouse stewardess)

George Smith, 1900–02 (steward)

Andrew Gazzalle, 1904 (from Burlingame Country Club)

Charles H. Singleton, 1910–24 (from New Zealand)

Edward A. Watson, 1924–30

George Stevenson, 1930–38 (from Sir Francis Drake and Clift Hotels)

Frank W. Harding, 1939–40

Walter H. Ramage, 1941–42

J. A. Ledward, 1942–45

Henry Ploennis, 1946–48 (from Detroit and Cleveland Navigation Company)

Cannon Lorimer, 1948–72

Irwin Kingsley, 1973–77

Carlo Bianchi, 1977–84

Michael Carabine, 1984–86

Alec Churchward, 1987–Present (from Orinda Country Club)

## Golf Professionals

James Melville, 1897–98 (from Scotland)

John G. Motion, 1889 (nine months only)

Horace Rawlins, 1899–00 (won first U.S. Open in 1895)

Willie Anderson, 1900–01 (from Baltusrol; won four U.S. Opens: 1901, 1903–05)

George Smith, 1902–13 (son of James "Pop" Smith)

John Lambie Black, 1913–23 (tied for second in 1922 U.S. Open)

J. William Fries, 1924–26

Eliot Callender, 1927 (returned to Monterey Peninsula Country Club)

J. Dewey Longworth, 1928–60 (from Kansas City Golf Club)

Talbert C. Smith, 1960–80 (won California State Open in 1946)

John Fite, 1980–99 (was assistant pro under Tal Smith)

Jay McDaniel, 1999–Present

## Greenskeepers

R. Bruegger, 1898–02

James "Pop" Smith, 1903–08 (designed original golf course)

Louis Galletti, 1908–56

Arthur Graziano, 1957–72

Stanley Burgess, 1973–78

Randy Gai, 1978–Present

## Tennis Professionals

Tom Stow, 1931–41

Patrick O'Hara, 1942–64

E. Martin "Blackie" Jones, 1965

Dennis Burchell, 1966–68

Mike Sheridan, 1969–70

John Hilton, 1970–95

Paul Garron, 1995–98

Steve Shaw, 1999–Present

## Swimming Pool Managers

Henry "Hank" Squires, 1950–75

Al Thurling, 1976–85

Karen Thurling, 1985–Present

## Chefs

(many names are missing)

Jean Douat, 1952

Fritz A. Bauer, 1965–74

James Hensley, 1975–76

Ralph Doyle, 1977–78

Fritz A. Bauer, 1978–81

Ronald Chritchley, 1982–97

Robert Gee, 1997–Present

## Golf—Men
## Club Championship Winners

| | |
|---|---|
| 1919—J. F. Neville | 1962—Ted Engs |
| 1920—F. A. Kales | 1963—Don Haslett |
| 1921—W. P. Gaddis | 1964—Vern Goodwin |
| 1922—F. A. Kales | 1965—R. G. Stevenson |
| 1923—F. A. Kales | 1966—Richard Railsback |
| 1924—F. A. Kales | 1967—R. G. Stevenson |
| 1925—F. A. Kales | 1968—Harry Gibson |
| 1926—O. R. Morgan | 1969—Tim Howard |
| 1927—F. A. Kales | 1970—Jim Dickson |
| 1928—George Pickerell | 1971—Don Haslett |
| 1929—C. M. Price | 1972—Lee Wilson |
| 1930—C. V. Goodwin | 1973—Robert Sciutto |
| 1931—C. M. Price | 1974—Tim Howard |
| 1932—C. V. Goodwin | 1975—Jim Dickson |
| 1933—Stuart Heatley | 1976—William C. Helfrich Jr. |
| 1934—Thomas Telfer | 1977—Bill Celli |
| 1935—Thomas Telfer | 1978—Lee Wilson |
| 1936—Thomas Telfer | 1979—Don Haslett |
| 1937—Thomas Telfer | 1980—Dr. Alan Harley |
| 1938—Thomas Telfer | 1981—Samuel J. Lindamood Jr. |
| 1939—R. G. Stevenson | 1982—Michael S. Donovan |
| 1940—George Ehmann | 1983—Dr Alan Harley |
| 1941—C. V. Goodwin | 1984—John E. Bade Jr. |
| 1942—C. G. Morse | 1985—Christopher B. Woodward |
| 1943—W. A. Finlay | 1986—John E. Bade Jr. |
| 1944—C. G. Morse | 1987—John E. Bade Jr. |
| 1945—R. G. Stevenson | 1988—George H. Kelley |
| 1946—C. G. Morse | 1989—George H. Kelley |
| 1947—Donald Haslett | 1990—George H. Kelley |
| 1948—Donald Haslett | 1991—George H. Kelley |
| 1949—Donald Haslett | 1992—George H. Kelley |
| 1950—R. G. Stevenson | 1993—George H. Kelley |
| 1951—Weller Noble | 1994—George H. Kelley |
| 1952—Donald Haslett | 1995—George H. Kelley |
| 1953—Allan Ledford | 1996—Glenn R. Rogers |
| 1954—Carrel Weaver | 1997—Michael S. Donovan |
| 1955—Donald Haslett | 1998—Drew Y. Sanders |
| 1956—Donald Haslett | 1999—Randy Jones |
| 1957—Raymond Deston | 2000—Drew Y. Sanders |
| 1958—R. G. Stevenson | 2001—Drew Y. Sanders |
| 1959—Dick Keyser | 2002—Mark Maguire |
| 1960—Donald Haslett | |
| 1961—Donald Haslett | |

## Golf—Women
## Club Championship Winners

| | |
|---|---|
| 1925—Mrs. C. F. Ford | 1964—Miss Sally Tomlinson |
| 1926—Mrs. H. A. Prole | 1965—Mrs William Forman |
| 1927—Mrs. H. A. Prole | 1966—Mrs. Miles Griffin |
| 1928—Mrs. H. A. Prole | 1967—Mrs. Miles Griffin |
| 1929—Mrs. F. J. Reagan | 1968—Mrs. Miles Griffin |
| 1930—Miss Harriet Hume | 1969—Miss Sally Tomlinson |
| 1931—Miss Barbara Lee | 1970—Miss Sally Tomlinson |
| 1932—Mrs. Wyman Taylor | 1971—Miss Sally Tomlinson |
| 1933—Mrs. Wyman Taylor | 1972—Miss Sally Tomlinson |
| 1934—Mrs. C. B. Kenny | 1973—Miss Sally Tomlinson |
| 1935—Mrs. Wyman Taylor | 1974—Miss Sally Tomlinson |
| 1936—Mrs. A. Emory Wishon | 1975—Mrs. Miles Griffin |
| 1937—Mrs. Wyman Taylor | 1976—Miss Sally Tomlinson |
| 1938—Mrs. Wyman Taylor | 1977—Miss Sally Tomlinson |
| 1939—Miss Cynthian D. Pike | 1978—Miss Sally Tomlinson |
| 1940—Marie C. Dieckmann | 1979—Miss Sally Tomlinson |
| 1941—Mrs. Wyman Taylor | 1980—Miss Sally Tomlinson |
| 1942—Mrs. S. N. Parkinson | 1981—Mrs. Roberta Cords |
| 1943—Mrs R. E. Cotter | 1982—Miss Sally Tomlinson |
| 1944—Mrs. S. N. Parkinson | 1983—Mrs. Miles Griffin |
| 1945—Miss Elizbeth Elliott | 1984—Mrs. Bette Evans |
| 1946—Miss Elizbeth Elliott | 1985—Mrs. Pam Gregory |
| 1947—Miss Elizbeth Elliott | 1986—Mrs. Molly Crowley |
| 1948—Miss Elizbeth Elliott | 1987—Mrs. Molly Crowley |
| 1949—Miss Barbara Dawson | 1988—Miss Sally Tomlinson |
| 1950—Miss Elizbeth Elliott | 1989—Mrs. Molly Crowley |
| 1951—Mrs. G. Lovel Parker | 1990—Mrs. Molly Crowley |
| 1952—Mrs. G. Lovel Parker | 1991—Mrs. Charles Cords |
| 1953—Miss Elizbeth Elliott | 1992—Mrs. Molly Crowley |
| 1954—Miss Elizbeth Elliott | 1993—Mrs. Molly Crowley |
| 1955—Mrs. Miles Griffin | 1994—Mrs. Charles Cords |
| 1956—Mrs. LeRoy Krusi | 1995—Mrs. Charles Cords |
| 1957—Mrs. Victor K. Atkins | 1996—Miss Sally Tomlinson |
| 1958—Mrs. Miles Griffin | 1997—Miss Gigi Cronin |
| 1959—Mrs. Mahlon Jordan | 1998—Mrs. Pat Allen |
| 1960—Mrs. R. G. Stevenson | 1999—Miss Gigi Cronin |
| 1961—Mrs. William B. Forman | 2000—Miss Gigi Cronin |
| 1962—Mrs. Miles Griffin | 2001—Miss Sally Tomlinson |
| 1963—Miss Sally Tomlinson | 2002—Miss Sally Tomlinson |

## Golf—Men
## President's Cup Winners

| | |
|---|---|
| 1921—Fitzgerald Marks | 1963—Dick Keyser |
| 1922—B. J. Cantillon | 1964—Weller Noble |
| 1923—O. R. Morgan | 1965—Bill Marks |
| 1924—A. E. DeArmond | 1966—Roger W. Hackley, M.D. |
| 1925—C. E. Fleager | 1967—Bill Marks |
| 1926—J. B. Lumgair | 1968—Jim Dinwidde |
| 1927—P. J. Walker | 1969—Roger W. Hackley, M.D. |
| 1928—F. A. Kales | 1970—Jim Dinwidde |
| 1929—Norman McKee Lang | 1971—W. D. Bates |
| 1930—William Deans | 1972—Ed Foley |
| 1931—A. N. Selby | 1973—Kenneth G. Hecht Jr. |
| 1932—A. N. Selby | 1974—Don Haslett |
| 1933—Thomas Telfer | 1975—Harry Gibson |
| 1934—H. A Willoughby | 1976—Weldon Russell/Harry S. |
| 1935—E. B. von Adelung | Anthony* |
| 1936—L. D Terreo | 1977—Don Haslett |
| 1937—H. G. Meek | 1978—Roger W. Hackley, M.D. |
| 1938—R. G. Stevenson | 1979—George Hughes |
| 1939—C. G. Perkins | 1980—Bill Logan |
| 1940—George C. Ehmann | 1981—John Gruen III |
| 1941—William L. Oliver | 1982—William H. Banker |
| 1942—H. K Snively | 1983—M. Blair Hull |
| 1943—Weller Noble | 1984—Kent Penwell |
| 1944—Val Vallette | 1985—Kent Penwell |
| 1945—R. C. Hackley | 1986—Jerry L. Becker |
| 1946—R. G. Stevenson | 1987—Dave Fenton |
| 1947—George C. Ehmann | 1988—Monte Haslett |
| 1948—Don Haslett | 1989—Victor A. Hebert |
| 1949—Don Haslett | 1990—Page Van LobenSels |
| 1950—Don Haslett | 1991—Blair Hull |
| 1951—O. D. Hamlin Jr. | 1992—Victor A. Hebert |
| 1952—E. F. Becker Jr. | 1993—Allyn D. McAuley |
| 1953—Wallace M. Glosser | 1994—George C. Hill III |
| 1954—Sterling Myers | 1995—Matthew P. Moran |
| 1955—Herman C. Verwolert | 1996—Richard Haas |
| 1956—Harry Gibson Jr. | 1997—Peter E. Ragsdale |
| 1957—William Marks | 1998—Thomas Counts |
| 1958—Clay Bedford | 1999—Roger Huddlestone |
| 1959—John Donovan Jr. | 2000—Justin Roach |
| 1960—Ted Engs | 2001—Page Van LobenSels |
| 1961—Ted Engs | 2002—Bruce O'Neill |
| 1962—Ted Engs | *Best Ball Format |

## Golf—Women
## President's Cup Winners

| | | |
|---|---|---|
| 1933–Miss Marie C. Dieckmann | 1957—Mrs. Wyman Taylor | 1980—Mrs. John C. Lasher |
| 1934—Miss Anita Dieckmann | 1958—Mrs. John C. Lasher | 1981—Mrs. Arthur P. Crist III |
| 1935—Mrs. M. E. Keyser | 1959—Mrs. C. V. Goodwin | 1982—Mrs. Rudolph Bain |
| 1936—Mrs. S. E. Stretton | 1960—Mrs. Harry Gibson Jr. | 1983—Mrs. Lloyd Pfeifer |
| 1937—Miss Betty Ballachey | 1961—Mrs. William Barlow | 1984—Mrs. Tracy Cuttle |
| 1938—Miss Marie C. Dieckmann | 1962—Mrs. Thomas Witter | 1985—Mrs. Virginia Goodwin |
| 1939—Miss Jane Volkmann | 1963—Mrs. Miles Griffin | 1986—Mrs. William Banker |
| 1940—Mrs. Lyle Sampson | 1964—Mrs. C. V. Goodwin Jr. | 1987—Mrs. Marily Johnson |
| 1941—Mrs. Dorothy Forbes | 1965—Mrs. William H. Banker | 1988—Mrs. Frank Smith |
| 1942—Mrs. Andrew Christ | 1966—Mrs. Stephen Prescott | 1989—Mrs. Virginia Goodwin |
| 1943—Mrs. R. J. Bailey | 1967—Mrs. William S. Laidley | 1990—Mrs. William Channell |
| 1944—Mrs. Wyman Taylor | 1968—Mrs. Russell Griffin | 1991—Mrs. Beth T. Landis |
| 1945—Mrs. Robert Christ | 1969—Mrs. William H. Banker | 1992—Mrs. Meredith Stanten |
| 1946—Miss Anita Dieckmann | 1970—Miss Elizabeth Elliott | 1993—Mrs. Charles Cords |
| 1947—Mrs. Wyman Taylor | 1971—Mrs. John M. Evans Jr. | 1994—Mrs. Meredith Stanten |
| 1948—Miss Elizbeth Elliott | 1972—Mrs. Richard Stevenson | 1995—Mrs. Marcia Roemer |
| 1949—Mrs. P. O. Pedersen | 1973—Mrs. Don Hucke | 1996—Mrs. Pat Allen |
| 1950—Mrs. Emory Wishon | 1974—Mrs. Lynn J. Gillard | 1997—Mrs. A. P. Crist III |
| 1951—Mrs. Miles Griffin | 1975—Mrs. William Channell | 1998—Mrs. Pat Allen |
| 1952—Mrs. LeRoy Krusi | 1976—Miss Elizbeth Elliott | 1999—Mrs. Ardis Crist |
| 1953—Mrs. Allan Ledford | 1977—Mrs. Lloyd Pfeifer | 2000—Mrs. Betty Shapiro |
| 1954—Mrs. Victor Atkins | 1978—Mrs. Arthur P. Crist III | 2001—Mrs. Laura Blackman |
| 1955—Mrs. Mahlon K. Jordan | 1979—Mrs. John H. Tiedemann | 2002—Mrs. Christine Harbert |
| 1956—Mrs. Victor K. Atkins | | |

## Golf—Men
## Oak Tree Classic Winners

| | Low Gross | Low Net | | Low Gross | Low Net |
|---|---|---|---|---|---|
| 1985 | Jon Q. Reynolds | John J. Donovan Jr. | 1994 | George H. Kelley | Dick Kraber |
| 1986 | Michael S. Donovan | Richard Haas | 1995 | Dick Kraber | Gary Sitzman |
| 1987 | Michael S. Donovan | Harold V. Lauth | 1996 | Phil Rowley | Don Gehb |
| 1988 | George H. Kelley | Edwin K. Wood | 1997 | Michael S. Donovan | Richard Haas |
| 1989 | George H. Kelley | Douglas R. Drewes | 1998 | Drew Sanders | Ken Meyersieck |
| 1990 | George H. Kelley | Don Haslett | 1999 | Randy Jones | Bill Frizell |
| 1991 | George H. Kelley | Chris Woodward | 2000 | Chris Woodward | Bruce Pollock |
| 1992 | George H. Kelley | Harold V. Lauth | 2001 | Phil Rowley | Glenn Rogers |
| 1993 | Chris Woodward | Monroe Townsend | 2002 | Randy Jones | Tom Kelley |

*Claremont Country Club Board of Directors, left to right: Richard Kraber, Don Jones, Tom Crosby, President Warren "Chip" Brown, General Manager Alec Churchward (standing), Phil Sarkisian, Glenn Rogers, Jim Smith, and Kent Penwell.*

James Parry Wagener, who is known by his middle name, was born in Oakland, California, and grew up in Piedmont, where he attended public schools. Upon graduation in 1959 from the University of California, Berkeley, with a B.S. degree in business administration, he was commissioned a second lieutenant in the U.S. Army and served in the Armor Corps at Fort Knox, Kentucky.

In 1966 Wagener married Roberta "Betsy" Greenlee of Piedmont, and their wedding reception was held at Claremont Country Club. They have two married children, Sarah and Peter, and two grandchildren. The Wageners, who joined Claremont Country Club in 1977, are able to trace six generations of membership at the Club. Long before becoming a member, Wagener had caddied and played golf at the Club while he was in high school. He recalled that some of the members' bags were extremely heavy to carry. During the 1950s, many members used large, expensive golf bags, some of which were made of exotic leather, including elephant hide.

After two corporate careers as a sales and marketing executive, Wagener retired to devote more time to family, golf, and historical research and writing. In 2000 he authored a treatise of the *Interpretation of the Sketches of Joseph Kendall,* a painter who sailed from New York to California in 1849. Planning and writing the pictorial history of Claremont Country Club for the Club's Centennial Celebration has been his largest writing project, and it has been rewarding personally. Wagener is proud to have been named Claremont's Historian, and he hopes other members will feel the same calling in the years to come and continue to maintain the historical records of this fine Club.